KISSING IN THE CHURCH

A MEMOIR

MACDANA SELEÇON

Kissing In The Church

A MEMOIR

MacDana Seleçon

Edited by Dawine Yoshioka

Cover Design by Mariah Dixon

Interior Layout Design by J. Benjamin Young Sr.
2019 20/20 Vision Books

ISBN
188589162-8
EAN-13
97-8-1-885891-624

PRINTED IN UNITED STATES OF AMERICA

20/20 Vision Books, Inc
www.hisimagepublishing.com
www.2020VisionBooks.com

To Liz

Love

[illegible]

This book is dedicated to Mariah, Tina, Ernessa, Lorraine, Joshua, Sabrina, and Jojo. I love you.

CONTENTS

INTRODUCTION

Everyone has a creed they identify with.

We believe in God the Father
We believe in Jesus Christ
We believe in the Holy Spirit
And He's given us new life
We believe in the crucifixion
We believe that He conquered death
We believe in the resurrection
And He's comin' back again, we believe

-Newsboys

Let me explain from the bottom up.

My Body

My body has one destination: death. It is a temporary dwelling place for my eternal spirit.

My Soul

My soul is my mind, will and emotions. It is more powerful than my body, yet underutilized.

My Spirit

My spirit; pure Love, is the most beautiful part of me. It is the omnipresent God within me, within us.

Hi reader! Thank you for opening this book. I hope you will enjoy it. Before you dive in, I'd like to orient you to my writing.

When I started writing this book, the concept was to write and pinpoint events in my life that led to my brokenness. I decided to focus on my experiences and the lessons I learned. Each chapter is structured to stand alone as its own short story.

There are several moments in this book, where I have difficulty expressing my feelings. I can attribute that to a couple things. First, during my traumatic childhood, I suffered from a condition called dissociation, which is common in child abuse survivors.

Dissociation is a mental process that causes a lack of connection in a person's thoughts, memory and sense of identity. In other words, it's a defense mechanism that our body utilize to escape trauma. To be clear, my body was there but my mind had left the building because it could not bear.

Secondly, cultural concepts of distress. Coming from a Haitian-American background, a child expressing self was frowned upon and considered disrespectful. With that being said, you can now understand why it was so natural for me in certain situations to be slightly apathetic. I disconnected from my emotions.

In the Beginning....

About four years ago at the age of twenty-eight, I hit rock bottom. I was fired from one of many jobs, my car had been repossessed due to my lack of responsibility and Mom and I were no longer on speaking terms. To make life even more difficult, my apartment was taken over by mold and I now had to find other residence. I moved in with a friend and her family. They were zealots of the

Christian faith and God sent. I informed them of all my troubles and fears. Their suggestion; pray and fast for forty days. From seven am to seven pm, all I ate was the Word of God. I sat alone in a room with my bible open and my computer on. When I came across Luke 7:48 "and He said unto her, 'your sins are forgiven.'" It resonated with me. Through my writing, I confessed my sins and accepted His forgiveness. In that room, I was renewed. I felt ready to understand my self-destructive behavior tendencies. I desperately wanted to heal my inner child.

The root of my problem was the residual effects I suffered from being abused and neglected as a child. Writing is a powerful therapeutic tool. The healing began the minute I expressed my thoughts on paper and I pray it continues through you.

As my journey continued, I met people along the way and discovered my story was not unique. I am not alone. We all have troubles and even triumphs but we don't talk about it. After five years of prayer and support from close friends and family, I chose to share my story of shame, infirmities, struggles, failures and ultimately hope with you. Hope is the feeling that what is wanted can be had or that events will turn out for the best. With great faith I am confident my story will provide that to you.

The stage darkens and the noise of the crowd reduces to whispers. In that last minute before making her entrance she decides to kick off her shoes. She squeezes the microphone and prays her pounding heart will return to a normal rhythm. Then she said with a quiver in her voice, "Is this thing on?" The crowd chattered. Then a spotlight landed on her and startled everyone into silence. She inhaled and prayed again; this time that her trembling hands would relax. "Hello, my name is MacDana, like a Big Mac and a Dana put together." The crowd laughed. She smiled. "My last name is Seleçon, which actually means... the lesson."

CHAPTER 1

ONCE UPON A TIME

There is a picture out there somewhere. My mother keeps it. I bet she still stores it in her big black suitcase. It is like a Barney bag, filled with an endless collection of Hallmark cards received for birthdays and holidays. Tons of letters, receipts, birth certificates, and a plethora of family photos. There is a picture of me at my worst, still one of Mom's favorites. I had to be about five or six-years-old. Mom sat on the ground to capture my entire body. I appeared tall and malnourished. I stood naked with baby powder splayed around my neck like a necklace and my hair sectioned into four big braids. I stared into the lens with bulging, unsmiling eyes. When did it become legal to develop nude photos of a minor? Perhaps, the camera was a Polaroid. As a matter of fact, I'm sure it was.

Over the years when I annoyed Mom she retaliated and called me frog eyes. She storied, "When I was pregnant with you a huge frog jumped into our living room and scared me almost to death. That is how you ended up with your eyes." Mom always had the funniest stories, but this one… not so much. Now Mom tells me, "Your eyes are beautiful!"

Have you ever sat on your bed wide awake in the middle of the night watching TV? Suddenly, an infomercial with African children floods the screen. Their sad faces pronounced by puppy-dog eyes, protruding rib cages and ballooned stomachs. You shake your head in disappointment. A melancholy song plays in the background, plucking the strings of your heart. Then a soft-voiced narrator explains the details of sponsorship. It hit me like a slap to the face; that Polaroid picture of me resembled these children.

FAMILY OR FOE

My mother birthed six children, and there was only one boy among us. My first two sisters were born in Haiti. Mom then migrated to the coast of Florida and conceived my older brother. A few years passed and she met my father. They conceived three daughters and I, MacDana, was in the middle.

Mom adored my father. She gushed about how well he threw an outfit together. Meanwhile, he relished any opportunity to introduce Mom as his lady. As is common in most relationships, things started off peachy; but not so common, were the moments when he transformed into Dr. Jekyll. No one knew he physically and verbally abused Mom.

My father grew up in a town in Haiti named *Port de Paix*, which, translates into Port of Peace. Ironically, Mom often said men from this particular town were notorious for beating their wives. I guess she gave my father the benefit of the doubt. Countless stories linger in her memory of the creatively cruel and unusual ways my father abused her. Beating her with his hands became his religion. Tearing her to pieces with words were his prayers. Some of the stories in this chapter belong to Mom. I included them in this book because the evolution of my life is a product of my parent's choices.

There is a timeless story about my mom, my dad and my godfather and I sitting at the dinner table. "Godfather of the year" decided to ask a few questions.

"*Cheri*, who do you love more: mommy or daddy?" I was three or four years old at the time of this interrogation. My feet swung happily under the dinner table as I picked at my meal.

"Mommy!" I exclaimed.

Obliviously he questioned further, "Why?"

"Because daddy beats mommy and I don't like it."

My father slowly pushed his chair away from the dinner table in a silent rage. He walked over to my seat and yanked me out of my chair. In front of my very pregnant mom and everyone else at the dinner table he gave me a beating which today would generate over a million views and angry emojis on YouTube. My godfather tried to intervene, to no avail. My siblings cringed in silence. Mom recalls crying, screaming and begging him to stop as the beating went on. In the midst of this pointless child abuse—he paused with annoyance and said to Mom, "If you continue to scream, I will make you deliver that baby in your stomach through your nose." Whenever Mom shares this story, I travel back in time with her and relive the horror.

Sadly, beatings were only the tip of the iceberg. Mom became his modern-day prisoner. Every day before leaving for work he drew a chalk line behind her rear tires. The lines served as indicators. After work, he'd crawl onto his hands and knees as he inspected her tires for evidence of departure. Living with my father became unbearable.

My youngest sister was unplanned. After confirming the pregnancy, Mom tried several home remedies to abort. Thankfully, her attempts were unsuccessful: *I love that girl*! Baby sister entered the world and Mom devised a plan to escape. She sold her car to a friend and only had enough money to purchase two one-way plane tickets to New York. She decided to take my brother with her, fearing he would be mistreated as a stepson.

I'M GOING TO NEED THAT PHOTO BACK

Father began seeing another woman. Unfortunately, the new woman didn't sign up to raise his three daughters. I'm uncertain why we became separated. My eldest sister stayed with my father and the new woman. My baby sister and I were given the boot; he drove us to a distant relative's home in Miami. He carried my baby sister, and I trailed behind him into their home. After a few empty promises, he returned to his car and drove off.

This next part of the story I will share with you, but I find it a bit difficult to remove my emotions. On the other hand, this is MY story, and I lived it, so I am entitled to feel "some type of way."

Our stay with these relatives changed my life forever. At five-years-old, I became a maid. I learned how to slide empty crates in front of their sink to stand on, while washing dishes and scrubbing pots. *Still, to this very day, I hate washing dishes.* When my duties were completed, I often sat in the backyard nibbling on grass. Your guess is as good as mine as to why I ate grass. Children do strange things after parental abandonment. Of this I am sure; I missed Mom even though she left me.

Unlike most daughters, I was a bona fide momma's girl. I remember at about three-years old I became very depressed when Mom went to the hospital for a few days to give birth to my sister. She left us with a sitter, who tried to console me, but nothing worked. At night, I fell asleep at our front door awaiting Mom's return. The sitter took me to my room. But the next morning she found me asleep at the front door again. When Mom heard about my behavior, she left the hospital against medical advice.

While living with those relatives in Florida, every morning when the sun graced the sky I entered the twilight zone of servitude. Nightly, as the moon illuminated the ocean, I entered a living nightmare. We slept in the kitchen, and our bed consisted of a single, thin-sheet draped on cold floor tiles. Our faux- bedroom faced an actual bedroom occupied by a pre-teen boy. At night, when everyone slept, his demons arose and I fell victim to them all. He fed his sexual curiosity with my five-year-old body every night. He shared his secrets with several boys in the neighborhood, and I met them all. I remember them as shadows. They entered through his bedroom window, and everyone had a turn. Nightmarish memories of those boys haunted me for many years. I saw them as they climbed through the window; black silhouettes without faces.

Mom settled in New York and immediately begun her search for us. Several phone calls later she learned my sisters and I were separated.

"Where are my babies?"

"They are doing much better than you," Dad lied.

Mom had no idea we were on the brink of being sent to Haiti or that my father had neglected his responsibilities. She didn't know that we lived in another abusive environment.

She bypassed my father's absurdities and asked everyone she knew in South Florida to search for us...and we were found.

Give me a second to pour out my love to God on this page. If it wasn't for your divine intervention, who knows what would have become of us. I love you and will spend the rest of my life giving thanks to you for near-misses. If a day should come and I am unable to speak your praises, God, I will lift my hands. When my arms grow weary, I will dance. When the day comes and my body is no more, my spirit will worship. The world will never comprehend the reason for my enthusiastic praise. It is only I who understands the reason why I sing.

Mom rushed back to Florida for us. When she walked into the room, I instantly forgave her and ran into her arms. Her tears caressed my face. She cried with relief and agony. My pronounced collarbone and bloated abdomen told Mom part of my story. My doctor told Mom another part. She cried as if what the boys had done to me every night had also happened to her. She cursed my father after realizing the situation he left us in. She despised him, and so did I.

I hated my father for breaking my heart. My foundation cracked with abandonment and sexual abuse. Each time those boys had sex with me, they left an infestation of filth which started my sexual addiction. Like a seed, it took root with choking collaterals, and grew within me. Suffocating. Mom thought my weeds were flowers. She stared at my naked photo without seeing anything at all.

S.O.S

Mom took us home with her. We lived in a one bedroom apartment located on Eastern Parkway. The famous Brooklyn Museum stood across the street. We were poor, but I was naive to it. To be with Mom again felt like a blessing. She, however, became a single provider for three children in the United States and two teenagers in Haiti. She worked long hours as a Home Health Aide and overtime as a mom. We always ate home-cooked meals for dinner. She fixed our plates before leaving for work while repeating her mantra, "Don't open the door for anyone, don't answer the phone when it rings, don't touch the stove, and don't leave the apartment."

Mom turned lemons into lemonade. As a child, I went crazy with joy about Christmas and presents. My favorite Christmas gift I received from Mom was a life-sized brown doll. She wore a pink dress speckled with white polka dots. I styled her shiny, black, curly-hair daily and sat her on the couch with me. She had big eyes, like mine. We were true friends.

Mom couldn't afford a babysitter to watch over us when she went to work so my brother inevitably became our sitter. *Children should not babysit children.* I turned six and the baby finally got potty-trained. He did a decent job as a big brother: warmed up our food, never answered the phone or the door, and he even gave us our baths. Unfortunately, he grew very curious about genitalia. It's fair to assume he found his penis. All little boys do that. Afterward, he found my vagina. He never had sex with me, but crossed the line, nonetheless.

As he played doctor with pure fascination, I froze on Mom's bed. He poked, probed and palpated. I found myself in the same position as before. But this time I knew the monster. I told him NO, but he continued. I hated it. He violated me in his ignorance.

Mom never knew what happened after bath time; I never told her. I couldn't; he scared me. Over time he turned into a volatile adolescent. He went in and out of juvenile prison for various charges. As I grew a little bit older and bolder, I put a stop to the fondling, and our relationship became explosive. He tortured me. One time he chased me around the house with a hairspray blow torch. I will never forget the day he walked into our apartment dangling a dead rat by its tail. I screamed at the top of my lungs and ran into Mom's closet and held the door shut with all my strength. My brother laughed and left the rat outside the closet. He removed it just before Mom arrived.

Mom worked late one night and asked our neighbor to take us to church. On our way to service, my brother started repeating everything I said with a nasally sound. Annoying. We went back and forth until our neighbor told him to quit. He begrudgingly did, only to sneak out during prayer to execute revenge. With a rock, he smashed the neighbor's car window into pieces. Then he walked home and submerged the house phone into a sink of water. His behavior worsened. Mom lost control and decided to send him packing to his father who lived in Florida.

If your children are tormenting one another, it is important to find out why. Sometimes it can be a mean spirit arising from a broken place. The real issue between my brother and I began when he violated my trust. I hated him for being the offender and, in return, he hated me for being the victim. Don't ignore or dismiss your children if they fight or argue. Get to the root of the problem. Ignoring it is foolish. Ask God to show you what is going on, and He will reveal it to you. Pray for them always. The children which God gave you are your responsibility. It is impossible to monitor them every second of every day, but your prayers can protect them.

You must also do the work and talk to your children. You can't pray away something you don't understand.

These rapes happened at such a tender age. The enemy likes to get them while they are young. When rape happens to a child it's much like the silent worm within the apple; gnawing away without a sound, going unnoticed as it destroys the victim to the core. The hole in the apple IS conspicuous, but you must be attentive in order to see it. Even with the damage, the fruit can be saved. Its seed can be replanted. As a child, I masked the pain like a feverish toddler who still wants to play. My mother could not see the pain or the damage, yet the evidence was clear.

CHAPTER 2
SEX AND RELIGION

We left Brooklyn and moved to Montclair, New Jersey. I started third grade, and our family attended a Haitian Pentecostal church in East Orange. I wasted little time before joining the youth choir. Singing fed my imaginations of stardom. Gospel songs and sappy love songs swirled in my mind throughout each day: Kirk Franklin or Celine Dion. On Sunday's before our choir performed, each member recited scripture into a microphone. Most of us shared one to two verses in English or French. Yes, it was a Haitian church, but most Haitian churches read from French Bibles, yet, the sermons are in Creole because they communicate in Creole. Some of us recycled well-known scriptures, "The Lord is my Shepherd, I shall not want." Others stammered over words due to stage fright.

Our family owned a Haitian Creole Bible. I challenged myself to read, memorize and recite from it. The church sat amazed by an American-born child's ability to share in a non-native tongue. I barely spoke Creole and Mom spoke minimal English. Nevertheless, we understood each other without much effort. The first day I grabbed the microphone and recited my half of a chapter in Creole, she peeked from underneath her church hat to witness my surprise performance. Soon after, I became a valued member of the youth choir and the pastor's favorite.

Six days to study several verses, or, cram it all in late Saturday afternoons? Waiting last minute to rush and study worked for me. Cramming made little sense, but I preferred it. Therefore, on Saturday's I sat behind Mom's bed, selected a passage between four to seven verses long and repeated out loud, verse after verse for hours. To interrupt the monotony, I entertained myself drawing and coloring with scented markers. Out of all the markers, Grape was my favorite. Just like my favorite Kool-Aid. Even with colorful caps on, they distracted me.

I hid between Mom's bed and a wall with a lonely window that faced another brownstone building. On cold-tiled floors in front of me rested the Holy Bible with black and red letters. In front of words spoken by Christ, I explored my vagina with markers. Curiosity transitioned innocent markers to sex toys. Mom never noticed, nor did she suspect me or my innocent markers. I stuffed one inside of me and walked around the house with it. Little girls keep secrets, and so did I. After this long session of studying and discovery, Mom asked to hear my verses in the kitchen as she finished cooking Sunday dinner. I took one last look at the words and recited proudly:

"Matye 7:1-5 Pa jije moun pou Bondye pa jije nou, paske Bondye va jije nou menm jan nou jije lòt yo. Mezi nou sèvi pou mezire lòt yo, se li menm menm Bondye va sèvi pou mezire nou tou. Poukisa pou w'ap gade ti pay ki nan je frè ou, epi ou pa wè gwo bout bwa ki nan je pa ou la? Ou menm ki gen yon gwo bout bwa nan je ou la, kouman ou ka di frè ou: Kite m' wete ti pay ki nan je ou la? Ipokrit! Wete gwo bout bwa a ki nan je pa ou la anvan. Apre sa, wa wè klè pou ou ka wete ti pay ki nan je frè ou la."

In English it reads…

Matthew 7:1-5 "Do not judge, or you too will be judged.For in the same way you judge others, you will be judged, and with the measure you use, it will be measured to you. Why do you look at the speck of sawdust in your brother's eye and pay no attention to the plank in your own eye? How can you say to your brother, 'Let me take the speck out of your eye,' when all the time there is a plank in your own eye? You hypocrite, first take the plank out of your own eye, and then you will see clearly to remove the speck from your brother's eye."

How appropriate.

* * *

Mom reunited with the first man she ever loved. He also fathered my two older sisters. They married, and he moved into our small two-bedroom apartment in New Jersey. Mom told me to call him Daddy (*ugh*).

Women, please stop forcing your children to call another man Dad, simply to make him feel welcomed. If the man is worthy, your children will eventually call him Dad on their own. Allow him to earn their respect as a father and as a man.

While Mom worked long hours in the city he watched TV and slept on the couch. One afternoon I walked past the living room and my eyes were drawn to the brown, floor model TV. The black and white picture punctuated with intermittent static, drew me like a moth to a flame. It was as if the actress entering the tub took my hand and sat me down to learn a brand-new way to masturbate. I can't say with certainty that he watched me watching the actress through lowered eyelids, but I saw the smirk on his face. *Brother, please!*

After watching this porn-star in a tub: markers were child's play. I descended into a different world with welcomed pleasure.

* * *

While seated in church one day I accepted a hand-written letter from a boy. It read, "Will you be my girlfriend...yes or no?" Those simple words sent me boy-crazy. We were both in middle school, but I was several months older. He reminded me of Casanova: young and charming. His parents had two teenaged daughters before he surprised them with his arrival. As an only son and the baby of his family, he lived the life every kid dreamt of. Designer-wear, fresh hair-cuts, and every new toy. After I checked "yes" and we became a couple, I spent hours daydreaming of his outfits and him. He continued to write after that first letter, and he'd chase me after church service. We'd run to the corner store and he'd use his allowance to purchase candy for us both. For my birthday, he gave me a beautiful gold bracelet. Later, when I discovered he stole it from his sister's jewelry box, I returned it. He suffered a week without phone privileges or T.V. because of that crime.

For Christmas, he repented and used his allowance to buy me a Giga pet. All the cool kids seemed to have Giga pets in 1997. For a while, all the girls in our choir had a Giga pet except yours truly. Mom refused to spend her single-parent dollars on silly toys. A Giga pet was an electronic pocket toy with a virtual pet within. As the owner, I kept the pet alive by feeding it virtual pebbles, cleaning virtual poop, and providing virtual petting. I mainly remember feedings. My pet had a bottomless pit for a stomach. The pet grew with time, and that pretty much sums up 1997's entire *joie de vivre.* Life before iPads; tough but simple! It revolutionized how we did church, especially during those predictable sermons.

Mom flew to Haiti to host my eldest sister's wedding. She could not afford airfare for my baby sister and me so we stayed behind with a close family friend. I loved her, and sometimes I wanted to call her mom. Her smile sent warmth to anyone who witnessed it. Her home invited everyone to make themselves comfortable. She allowed all children to play without many restrictions. For the most part, children who visited were raised by strict Haitian parents, therefore, well behaved. She had a huge basement full of toys and extra space. We bolted down the steps to this playpen minutes after giving her a kiss on the cheek. She stayed upstairs, listening and sharing with the young women of the church. They always told us to leave so they could continue "grown-up" talks. Laughter echoed in her home. I adored that house for all the obvious reasons, but, I especially loved it because while Mom witnessed my sister kiss her groom in Haiti, Casanova gave me my very first kiss in this house.

The hopeless romantic in me will forever remember the following details. It happened after Sunday evening service. As usual several children came over for a visit, and Casanova found me perched on the stairs. He ascended past me, and I followed him into an empty bedroom. The house buzzed with joy. No one noticed the scent of our raging pheromones as we sat side-by-side on a twin-sized bed. We stared at the T.V., but only saw each other. Finally, the moment I practiced with mirrors for so long, materialized -- a tongue wrestle. The wait to touch his lips never ached before our first kiss. We exchanged breaths, and my soul discovered wings to fly. We became insatiable and went nuts. We hid and kissed everywhere and anywhere. In the basement of any building or house, during the annual church trips to Dorney Park in PA, or Coney Island in New York, on the stairwell, you get the point. For a long time, kissing conveyed our love for each other when words failed.

My body changed overnight as puberty settled in. Boobs protruded out of a stick figure. I remember aches as they swelled within my chest; like teeth erupting from gums. Ready or not, my body prepared for womanhood. Change entered like a whirlwind, both physically and socially. Our family found another church because Mom no longer agreed with some of the teachings at our old church. Just like that, Casanova and MacDana were no longer sitting and k-i-s-s-i-n-g in a tree. I was devastated.

Another revival ripped through the Haitian-church community. A revival is much like a regular church service except a renowned preacher is invited to speak and worship music is more spirited. The main goal is to revive the people. It's easy to grow stagnant in church with the same speaker and the same music and sometimes recycled messages. A mega-Haitian Church hosted this revival in the heart of our community in Essex County. People traveled from near and far to attend. Late-comers stood in the isles.

Our family decided to attend. We prepared for revival with dresses, make-up, curling irons, and pantyhoses. My eldest sister frowned, but allowed me to select two items from her wardrobe. A brown jacket paired with a complementary blouse, accentuated my new adolescent additions. We arrived, but once again, the entire service was in Creole, and every seed fell on stony ground.

One of the greatest disservices in the Haitian Church in America is preaching the gospel to an Americanized ear in a foreign tongue.

The sermon bored me. I distracted myself with people-watching. "Woman. Man. Boy. Teenage girl. Baby resting on woman's shoulder. Old woman with a scrunched face. Very old man smiling. Perhaps very old man released a silent air biscuit and the old woman smelt it. Gross! Now I have a scrunched face. But, I don't smell anything. Un-scrunch your face MacDana!" Time flew by until it stopped. I saw a familiar face. My insides stirred in a butterfly type of way. I stared and hoped the connection we shared would whisper, "She is here. Look left."

Dear God, please make him look this way. I prayed. He looked, and I turned away.

We lived towns apart with no way to meet each other. I cried after we left our old church until missing him stopped tearing me apart. Our secret phone calls got me into trouble. He called and rang once several times a day. After the coast cleared of all adults in my home, I returned his call. We loved being on the phone with each other while doing our chores or studying. He listened as I serenaded him with a Celine Dion song I rehearsed. He always said, "I love you" at least five times during our calls. And I loved him. Soon we talked less but loved the same.

Imagine my delight, to sit in church with him one last time. He stood, and I sat up straight. He made his way down the aisle, towards the back. I waited a few minutes and asked Mom for permission to use the bathroom. She nodded yes, and I followed his steps. Apparently, the sermon was captivating, for both our parents missed the sequence of events.

He waited for me at the bottom of the steps. We found an empty room and filled it with our love for each other. *The congregation shouted "Hallelujah!"* There we stood: kissing in the church. The clicking of high-heeled shoes walking towards our door separated us with fear. When their sound diminished in the distance he unbuttoned my brown jacket. *The congregation shifted to the edge of their seats.* I searched his eyes and they begged for more, for all of me. He loosened the buttons of my sisters' shirt, cupped my left breast, and every cell of my being vibrated. *The congregation gasped with anticipation.* He pressed my back against the wall. *The congregation stood with enthusiasm.* Then the door swung open, and a faithful usher appeared. *The congregation lifted their hands.* We bolted passed her, hiding our faces as I buttoned my shirt. *The people shouted one last "Hallelujah!"* We laughed with fear, love, and excitement.

Mom never heard about what happened in the church. Instead, she later intercepted one of our letters and spanked me like I stole something. A valuable lesson learned; letters are bad news for one's love life.

CHAPTER 3

RULES ARE NOT MEANT TO BE BROKEN

The two sisters of mine who grew up in Haiti had recently moved to the States. There was an eight to nine-year age gap between us and they spoke Creole, understanding only a few words of English. But just when I was starting to get to know them, Mom pulled the rug out and shoved it into a moving truck saying, "The cost of living in Georgia is more affordable than New Jersey, so, we are heading south." My sisters stayed behind and started their own families.

Furniture and moving boxes were crammed into a U-Haul truck headed for College Park, Georgia. Middle school ended, along with many friendships. I left every friend from first grade to eighth grade, behind. Mom did not allow me to use our house phone to make personal calls. Therefore, any hopes of staying in touch went out the window. Thank God for Myspace, a social network before Facebook, which later allowed me to reconnect with many of my Jersey friends.

My entire world changed overnight, and it scared me. I cried alone. Mom wasn't the sympathetic type; a weeping child annoyed her. She'd ask a few inappropriate-rhetorical questions like: "Do you have bills to pay, a mortgage, or a car note? Then, what is the problem?" At least she paused for a response before concluding with a threat, "Fix your face or I will give you something to be sad about."

When we left Jersey, besides leaving my friends, saying farewell to my favorite uncle on the planet pained me. I called him "Tonton," which means uncle in Creole. He had a head full of silly riddles and a way with Mom. I lost count of how many punishments he rescued me from. We enjoyed long walks during the summer. As we walked to the local Pathmark supermarket, I tucked my hands into his, while skipping and singing, "Don't step on the crack or you'll break your mama's back."

He earned a living as a car mechanic and often lugged his tools from New York to New Jersey to keep our family's Japanese-hooptie, running. Whenever he worked on Mom's car, I sat waiting for something cool to help with. "Real women know how to take care of their cars," he said. He allowed me to help change tires. I stepped onto the wrench, jumped up and down until the nuts loosened. Tonton smiled at my unconventional methods. We changed Mom's brake pads together. From under the car, he reached his oil-stained hand out, and I slapped whatever tool he requested into it. Tonton gave me latex gloves to wear to prevent my nails from blackening with grease, like his.

Tonton also gave me my first driving lesson. He had too much faith in my ability to follow directions under stress. "Now turn the wheel left. The other left. Turn the wheel faster! NO!" I heard him say turn the wheel, but my right foot pushed the gas pedal, and we collided into a building. I dented his bumper. Tonton remained calm and took over. I apologized many times, and he assured me everything was fine. He laughed and teased me. Then he said, "You did a good job. Don't worry about this old car. And let's not tell my crazy sister."

Driving cars and repairing them stumped me, but I excelled academically. Honor-roll grades decorated my report cards, and Tonton loved it. He studied my report card, stared me square in the eyes and said, "You make our family very proud, *Cheri*." Then he'd pull out his wallet and hand me a twenty-dollar bill. Other times he took me shopping and once surprised me with my very first pair of name-brand sneakers. They were white and grey with a hint of pink and huge letters which read FILA. The morning I went to school wearing those brand-new babies was...wait for it..., legendary! My right foot hit the pavement off the school bus and all the students in Mount Hebron Middle School gasped with shock. "That's right, your girl upgraded from Pro Wings to FILA's! Don't hate: congratulate!" *At least that is how it all went down in my head.*

I fell in love with him, like a daughter loves her dad. On the weekends, he rang our doorbell and I sprinted to the door, swung it open, bounced, squealed and wrapped all of me around his presence. I covered his face with kisses and asked, "Did you bring me anything?" He always did. After expending all my energy I'd find my favorite seat on his lap. There I nuzzled into his chest and listened to his steady heartbeat. *People often say all good things must come to an end...I hate that stupid saying. Especially when it rings true.* One day Mom observed our interaction as she shuffled around and blurted, "It is inappropriate for young ladies to sit on the laps of grown men. Get down! He is your uncle, not your father!" Mom made every law in our home. The new rules left me confused and ashamed. Just like that, reality changed again.

***

College Park, GA turned out to be alright; much prettier than our neighborhood in Montclair, N.J. Manicured trees welcomed us into our two-bedroom, carpeted townhouse. Mom had more space to decorate with fancy furniture. We had a huge kitchen with an island and sliding glass doors which opened to an enclosed patio. Our new community also included two swimming pools, running trails, and several playgrounds. My little sister and I shared a huge bedroom adjacent to Mom's bedroom. We had a white metal bunk-bed; she slept on the top bunk and me on the bottom. Mom made our sleeping assignments. A wooden dresser stood across the room with a TV and radio atop. I loved our minimalist décor. It left enough space to hold live solo or duet performances for a small audience in the empty space between the bed and the dresser. Often, it was only me standing in the center of the faux-stage squeezing the life out of the remote control; singing into it like a microphone that carried my voice out to the thin air around me as if the room was full of loyal fans.

Tonton came to visit us in G.A after we settled into our new home. I didn't think I'd see him again. I could not contain my joy. It was nice to see a familiar face, especially his. School was out for one of the holidays, which concluded with fireworks. Mom cooked all her finger-licking dishes: baked macaroni au gratin made with gouda cheese and evaporated milk; potato salad made with eggs, bell peppers, onions, and more mayo than mustard; *djon-djon* (mushroom) rice with shrimp; *griot* (fried pork) served with *pikliz (*shredded cabbage, mixed with carrot, scotch bonnet peppers and vinegar), and *poule en sauce* (stewed chicken in a tomato sauce) topped with sweet onions, and assorted bell peppers. We all had seconds. Then fireworks ended our festivities, and everyone prepared for bed.

The sleeping arrangements were different because Tonton was in town. Mom fixed a comfy floor palate for Tonton on my stage. First, she piled two comforters onto each other, then covered them with a thin floral sheet for aesthetics. Before her exit, she fluffed two pillows and threw them at Tonton. She unfolded a fleece blanket and dropped it on his make-shift bed. Little sister and I read each other's minds, "SLEEPOVER, YES!" She scurried to her top bunk, grabbed her favorite blanket. I met her near him giggling. She nestled into his right armpit, and I placed my head on his left chest. We cozied together center stage. Mom left the light on in the hallway and, like a harsh spotlight, it illuminated our three bodies next to each other. His hands rubbed our heads until baby sister snored softly. I tried to stay awake, to prolong our time together. His loving presence in our room was the best gift two fatherless girls could ask for. Yet, the sound of his baritone voice and my belly full of carbs lured me to sleep. My eyes surrendered. The curtains closed and everything faded to black.

Rewind Act One: the moment before the sun chased the stars and the moon out of the sky, before I blankly stared at the wall as I sat on the toilet for hours, before I flipped the light switch on and locked the bathroom door with dread, before I crawled from the set and escaped his betrayal, before my eyelids opened and my heart raced violently within my chest, before I silently screamed in horror, before his thumb and index finger twisted and turned my nipple, before my body grew tense with displeasure, before his left hand broke the barrier of my pajama shirt, before my eyelids surrendered to blissful fatigue, before my head nestled into his loving arms, before my favorite uncle who was more like a father to me, broke all the rules.

Mom was onto something when she said, "no more sitting on your uncle's lap." Perhaps she threw her commandment out of the window, or maybe she forgot with holiday cheer. Whatever the reason: rules are not meant to be broken. He was downgraded from "favorite uncle" to "we share DNA." We never talked about it. He stopped visiting. Who needed a dad anyway? The whole daddy thing wasn't working out for me. I never told Mom what her beloved brother did. I feared she wouldn't believe me; our family would be ruined; Uncle might lie; everyone would hate me. I placed a veil on my grief and smiled with teeth for Mom.

CHAPTER 4

CUZ

Blood is thicker than water. True, but blood is about 80 to 90 percent water. With all things considered, let me introduce you to Cousin. We weren't related via DNA, yet she was more than *just* a friend. We were barely close in New Jersey, but when our families became next-door neighbors in Georgia, our bond quickly formed. I admired her from the inside-out. Walking down the street with her was dangerous at times for drivers passing by. Men honked horns, pressed brakes, and rolled down their windows to shout, "Yo shawty," for her attention. She was 5'7", lean, with perfect posture. I was only three inches shorter, but my slouched shoulders gave her more height. She had a rounded mahogany face, modest almond eyes, Toni Braxton cheekbones, full lips, and a girlish smile. Bangs were an enemy to her face; her excellent features didn't require accessories. She often styled her hair like Halle Berry with boy shortcuts to match her preferred no-nonsense look. She was fierce.

Entering a new High School is an expected challenge for most freshmen. Yet, for me, it was easy because my sidekick was a senior who often ate with me during lunch period. Her upperclassman status gave me cool-points by association. She was often a safety net when my smart mouth got out of hand, and my peers wanted to pull out my hair. I was a mediocre fighter since I'd never fought anyone before, but she was sacrificial, ready to take my place in the ring. We were more than friends or cousins. She was a sister to me in every way possible. The only reason I named her Cousin was to keep my other four sisters from being jealous. It didn't work.

***

Cousin accepted me for whoever it was I wanted to be on any given day. Although I was a handful of crazy, she loved it all. The day I lost my keys in our community pool, she won the award for, Best Cousin Ever! I was known for losing any and everything; always losing my house keys (*still a present-day problem*). Finally, Mom said, "The next time you don't come home with your keys I will bang your head against every wall in this house." For some strange reason, she refused to believe the keys and I were playing hide and go-seek. "Is that really necessary?" I thought, "head trauma over keys? Wow!"

A few days later Cousin and I went to the pool after finishing our chores and I tucked both keys into my bathing suit top, it was *impossible* for them to escape, right? After several hours of swimming, we decided to go home before sunset. Careful cousin urged me to check for the keys. I did, only to realize they were gone. My heart dropped with fear. I was certain the escapees were at the bottom of our vast community pool. Hide and go seek was in full effect. Cousin decided to play. She searched the pool's vents twice, and every square inch of its floor. Surprisingly, she surfaced with one key and hope for the other. *Before YOLO became a popular saying amongst millennials: there was me!*

"What are you doing?" she asked. "Your keys are lost, stupid, not mine."

"Face it Cousin," I said while walking to the deep end of

the pool labeled 'no diving,' "There's no way we're gonna find the other key. My mom is going to kill me, but before I die, just one last swim." I inhaled deeply, and belly flopped into the deep end. The sun crawled around the globe and the other key remained lost. We walked home, silent and slow. Dread rendered two teenage girls mute for the very first time. I tried to brace myself for the promised concussions. We went to her house to change clothes in a last-minute delay tactic. As we peeled off our wet bathing suits, Cousin looked across the room and asked, "MacDana, what is that?" She pointed to my left chest.

"What?" I panicked and swatted my chest assuming it was a bug. But then the missing key fell onto the carpet. I looked at the key and then sheepishly at her. She was smiling and shaking her head. I started giggling. Eventually, we laughed until our bellies ached.

***

Cousin was a great listener, too. Listening to me tell a story requires a patient soul, someone who's willing to endure the dramatizations, hand gestures, reenactments, voice changes, props and emotional peaks required for an impromptu monologue. She endured rambling sessions, mindless gossip, she knew the details of my hopes and dreams and she guarded my fears with lock and key. She was my human diary.

Cousin,

Yesterday, the strangest thing happened. As I sang in the shower someone opened the bathroom door without knocking. I was sure it was my annoying little sister, but when I pulled back the shower curtain and stuck my head out to kick her out, I couldn't, because it wasn't her. It was *him,* my stepdad! He didn't say a single word, he only smiled. I pulled the curtain shut and prayed for him to hurry and leave. Then I heard him peeing in the toilet. What was that all about? There is a perfectly fine bathroom downstairs. Why couldn't he use that one? He makes me nervous cousin.

Thanks for listening.

Cousin,

Today Mom left me a ton of chores to do around the house. When did I become a slave? All I ever do is clean, clean, and clean. The house isn't dirty, yet I'm always cleaning. This is so unfair, why me? While I was in the kitchen wiping the *clean* counters my stepdad strolled in. I'm not sure why but he scares me. Why do I have to call him "daddy" when I can't stand him? He's only good for three things: watching TV, napping and eating. Where are his chores? He should have chores. He walked to the refrigerator, opened the door and grabbed a bottle of Prestige beer. Before going back to his man cave, he paused behind me, pushed his chest against my back and pressed his penis on my butt. Gross! Who does that cousin? I turned around and pushed him off me. He smiled and went upstairs. What did he find so funny? What a creep! I'm living with a pervert. I hate him!

Mom loves him. I want to tell her, but how? She went to Haiti and brought him here in the name of love. So what, he fathered my two older sisters. I love them but not him. Who cares if he was her first love? She has no clue how disgusting he is. He is not my father. He's not my blood. He doesn't care about us. She should have never moved him in here. Why didn't she talk to us first? I have so much to say…but no one ever asked me.

Thanks for listening.

Cousin,

Tomorrow is here! He is finally gone. I'm free of him, and I didn't have to say a single word. He did all the talking. Here is how it happened... Mom sat upstairs working on her sewing machine while he watched T.V. My sister did her homework in our bedroom and I did mine in the kitchen. He came down and sat across from me at the kitchen table. I looked up to see what he was doing, and there he was stupidly staring at me with a creepy smile that made me want to crawl out of my skin. I rolled my eyes, shook my head and continued reading. Then he said, "Your mom is crazy. She talks too much. She doesn't understand you the way I do. Don't worry you can always talk to me. You don't have to listen to her, just come to me. We are close, right? I will do anything for you. I love you baby and blah, blah, blah." I stopped paying attention when he opened his mouth.

As he blabbered, Mom tiptoed down the stairs like the pink panther and listened to his nonsense. She heard and understood everything, spoken and unspoken. She walked into the kitchen and said, "Well let me get this straight, you're trying to fuck my daughter? I worked so hard to bring you into the United States, and this is how you repay me? My daughter, you piece of shit, and in my house!" There was a knock at the door. "Oh, I have something for you *papa kochon* (father of pigs)." She answered the door, and two police officers stood outside. Can you believe it? Mom called them herself! She told them he was trying to have sex with me and they escorted him out. Mom asked me what seemed like a million questions afterward. I told her everything I told you. She said, "He will never come back to this house again." I can't believe she chose me over him, woohoo! Ding dong the weirdo's gone!

Thanks for listening.

***

Mom was my new hero. She didn't think twice when deciding, "Kids before pigs." Unfortunately, some parents drop the ball and make the wrong choice. It wasn't easy saying goodbye to her lover, her husband, her first kiss, and her friend. The depth of love lost escaped me. She descended into rage, and it caught me off guard. Something was terribly wrong. Mom stood in the tub fully dressed, scrubbing the tiles. She was doing my chores. With a customary kiss on the cheek I greeted her; all the while my insides were crumbling with fear. "Hi Mom, how are you?"

"What is this *kaka (*shit) you are wearing?" I looked down at my outfit, confused. "Your pants are too tight." For some strange reason, she was shouting. "These tight clothes are the problem. Did I send you to school to be a whore? If you weren't dressed like a slut all the time, tempting my husband, he would still be here. *Manman bouzin, map regle avec ou* (mother of bitches, I will deal with you)!" I was wearing fitted black slacks over coca cola hips; size 32 D breasts and a slim waist all outlined in a t-shirt. A mindless teen trapped in a grown woman's body.

Why didn't she punch me in my face, and repeat? I felt like her favorite pin cushion seated near her sewing machine. Her words like the many pins stabbing through me. Sticks and stones can break bones and words turn hearts into stone. Physical pain would've been less painful. I wanted her lover to return. I also wanted a different Mom. She shoved me aside and went into her bedroom, grabbed her shears from her sewing table and stormed into my room. She opened my closet and reached in. I stood near the door, watching with blurred vision and paralyzed in horror. When did these tears show up? Who was this woman sent to mother me? She hates me because the man she loved wanted me. I remember this moment in slow motion. She yanked my favorite butterfly dress from its hanger: a gift from my uncle, and turned it into rags, a pleated blue and white skirt with its matching top; rags, another pair of perfectly-fitted black pants, rags; Jordache jeans; rags. Snip and rip, snip and rip, snip and rip and repeat. She spoke words to destroy me and flung the pieces of me and the rags behind her. "Take off your pants!" I quickly fumbled out of my favorite pants and hurried to her with panties and a t-shirt on. Snip followed rip, and black rags were added to her pile. It ended when I had nothing left to wear. I stood naked and empty. She needed me to feel her pain, but all pain is not created equal. She needed revenge and succeeded. "Clean this up and throw it in the dumpster outside." I tossed the rags and all respect I ever had for her and me, and walked away.

Cousin,

What day is it? My head still aches from crying too much. May I borrow some of your clothes for school tomorrow? I don't have anything to wear. I hate her. Why couldn't I have been adopted? Why can't I stop crying? It hurts so much, my heart that is. I'm all in pieces. Thank you, cousin, I really needed a hug. If it's okay with you, may I continue to rest my head on your lap until my tears run dry?

Thanks for listening.

CHAPTER 5

IF YOU SAY I AM THEN I AM

Words

Hundreds on this page, thousands in this book

Spoken and untouchable, invisible and scentless

Yet, when a heart shifts and a tongue slips, oceans climb high, and mountains sink low

Words

We shared one temple, nine months

Submerged in her womb, nine months

Slept under her heart, nine months

Words

Begged me to crawl

Convinced me to stand

Her words cheered when I walked

Words

To her lyrics, I bounced

The paperweight, she kept me grounded

The catalyst, she changed me

Words

Regret "I should have murdered you."

Shame "I want nothing to do with you."

With fury she renamed me

A slut and A whore

Detestable, A bitch.

Words
Stood behind me
A patient crow, hungry
I ran between the raindrops
Her words soaked me
Slut? Reluctantly, but… now that's me
Hoe? I don't know, but… I guess so
Words
Mispronounced, she sounds like a stranger
Mom tell me who I am, in the midst of your anger
I'm standing in traffic with your words in my ear
Shall I stop or go, am I a daughter or a foe
Words
I hate you,
Mom lied.
Words
I love you,
He lied.
Another man inside me
Naked but ugly
Tattooed in graffiti
Black ink knocked over me
Strangely
She never wanted me to be, empty words, she cursed me
Reverse psychology failed me
Pavlov un-train me
The same letters which raised me
Rearranged, swords butchered me
Still, words won't relent, to build me up in the end.

CHAPTER 6
STRANGER DANGER

Our family attended a Seventh Day Adventist church in GA, and of course I joined the youth choir. We performed once a month, and it was our Saturday to take center stage. I squeezed the microphone and sang the solo part of our ensemble, and a man leaned forward for a closer look. I heard Mom's applause in the crowd and I saw her smile when our song ended. Ovations graciously ushered us off stage, and I sat in an open back pew. Coincidently, I sat directly in front of the strange man. He waited a few minutes into the church announcements before making his move. He leaned forward, tapped my shoulder and whispered, "Excuse me, child, my name is…, and do you know a woman named…, and a man named…?" Of course, I knew both names… they were my parents. After the benediction, I introduced him to Mom. *We are always one decision away from changing the entire course of our lives.* When I look back at this simple encounter, I wished I shouted, "CUT," followed by, "TAKE TWO!"

Man: Excuse me, child. My name is …, do you know a woman named …?

Me: Never met her.

Man: What about a man named …?

Me: Never heard of him.

Man: You look just like her.

Me: Oh, so now *all* black people look alike. Amazing! (Exit pew, quickly)

As we approached Mom, her eyes widened, "*Mezanmie, se pa mon frere*? What are you doing in Georgia?" They embraced each other joyously. Mom said he was as an old friend from Florida. They lost touch when she moved to New York. Recently, he relocated to Georgia for work and a friend invited him to our congregation. The sanctuary was nearly empty when Mom insisted he join us for dinner. He accepted.

He lounged in his grey dress socks in our dining room as he shared stories of a family, (my family that is) I could not remember. It appeared my parents were once crazy in love. "*Ma seour,*" he said. "All the children look just like you, especially your daughter in Florida." Mom's smile faded. The comment soured the moment. Mom felt obligated to explain why her mini-me remained with my dad and why she had not seen her in over ten years. "I didn't want to leave her," she said. "Mothers should raise children, but they did not give me a choice. She was always a difficult child and madly in love with her dad. I arrived at the house to pick her up, but when she realized it meant leaving her daddy she ran into a room and locked the door. I begged her to open it. She stood silently behind it, despite my crying. Her dad and his new girlfriend forced me to leave. By the time, I returned to New York their contact information changed."

The stories continued: now Mom narrated. She filled in the gaps for him. Even though he was a friend of my parents when they were a couple, he did not know the details behind their separation. Mom shared the long version of the years she spent secretly enduring my dad's physical abuse and formulating her getaway plan. To justify her hatred, she sacrificed my dignity, humiliated me and divulged my story of rape for what I hoped would be the last time. *It was not.* Mom harbored endless resentment for my dad. She used her tongue as vengeance. She told every open ear his sins. Our old family friend felt sorry for us. In a failed attempt to heal old wounds, he left a working phone number for my dad and sister. She stared at the numbers for several days and weighed each potential outcome. She wanted to speak to her daughter. Then she dialed 954… my dad answered, "*Alo*," and the fan got dirty.

"Hello," turned into an invitation. An invitation turned into a plane ride. A plane ride turned into two knocks on our front door. I opened it, and a stranger walked into our living room. His skin was a dark shade of brown. His jet-black hair neatly combed. He was short for a man and stood straight but slightly hunched over, *just like me.* I was afraid for a few deep breaths and then anger materialized fear. He smiled confidently and opened his arms for a hug, "MacDana, my daughter!" I almost met the proper greeting custom when I walked to him with heavy feet, kissed his cheek, but declined the hug invitation.

Why didn't I join the baseball team at school, I thought. *If I had, a baseball bat would be leaning against the wall inside our coat closet; patiently waiting to commence batting practice on his face. Did he just call me his daughter? Did sperm donation make you a father? Well then father, where were you when they ran a train on me at five? I see your lips moving, stale air blowing from your mouth, but I do not hear an apology. Until you beg on bloody knees for our forgiveness, someone, please show Father Useless the door.*

No one showed him the door. Instead, he and Mom walked

upstairs and she opened the door to her heart once again. They transformed into two giddy teenagers in lust. Now I wanted to finish batting practice on Mom's head.

When his visit ended, they kissed each other goodbye, the way lovers kiss. Goodbye translated into "see you soon." He returned to Florida and continued to call her. Mom found new joy in his attention. Eventually, phone conversations became unsatisfying and distance deepened their fondness for each other. Summer arrived, ninth grade ended, and two moving trucks loaded with our furniture went south on I-95 to greet my dad in Florida. Mom, sister and I followed in a Greyhound Bus.

I am a rag doll, and I belong to a deranged owner.
She drags me from place to place in search of the wind. She squeezes me till my eyes bulge out; she bends me in search of her spine. She pulls me as she falls apart. She shakes me as her foundation rocks. She screams but I can only stare. She pours her tears in my hair. She cries until I drown. She smiles and puts me down.
I am a rag doll, and I belong to a deranged owner.

We lived in G.A. for only a year, yet I mourned because I did not want to make new friends at a new school, find my place in a new church or live in a new home with another father. Fear of the unknown mixed with the weight of goodbye tormented me. I felt so many emotions, but the greatest was anger. I was angry with Mom for forcing my father into my life. She spent years reminding me and any open ear of how awful he was. Her sudden change of heart did not make any sense. She forgave him hastily; meanwhile, I struggled to call him "Father." I did not want to reconcile. Everything changed without a family meeting or full consideration.

We filed into the bus and found three seats towards the rear. I sat several rows closer to the front than Mom and my little sister. I got as comfortable as one could get on a greyhound bus. I stuffed my backpack under my seat, fluffed my pillow, and draped my blanket across my lap. As everyone claimed his or her seats, I stared out the window. The aisle seat right beside me remained empty until a young man sat down. Mom stood. She tiptoed and swayed side to side while holding the chair for balance. "MacDana, are you okay?" she said. I looked back and nodded yes. His mystique briefly captured my attention, but the window was awaiting my company. His presence made Mom uneasy, but our bus was at maximum capacity and ready for departure. Mom's intuition was always noteworthy, but this time she capped the pen too early. Begrudgingly, she sat down and relented.

He waited until late evening when most passengers gave into exhaustion to confirm her gut feeling. I allowed it to happen. His name…I did not know. His age…who cared? We barely spoke words but he heard "yes," from my body. "Yes, I want to be loved, by anyone who can hear me. It made no difference who, or where, or how. One sign of affirmation will do. One minute of affection will numb the pain. One more touch from one more man will cure it all. One more, please, just one more." When he slid his hands back into his own lap, I took one more step into an abyss called self-destruction.

CHAPTER 7

WELCOME BACK

Let the games begin! My father and I slept under the same roof again. We spent nine years separated by miles, now white walls divided us in our new, but outdated two-bedroom, one bath, tiny apartment. Within our compartmentalized-box, we played a game of House. He played the father, and I, the daughter. Our apartment was too small for the four of us. We smiled with our teeth and sheltered our hearts. Our greetings were cordial and vapid. "Good morning Dad." Calling him Dad was tolerable, but to call him Daddy would imply he was dear to me. He's was not.

Dad sat straight with perfect posture, briefly. He embodied his role as if it were an innate talent. Eventually, the mild curvature of scoliosis in his back bent into its preferred position. Gradually, he slouched. It required genuine effort to be a daddy and a mate. He only needed 10,000 more hours of holding his core, depressing his shoulders, elevating his chest, and extending his neck. After all, practice makes perfect: but Dad disliked repetition. Once, maybe twice, he hugged me. I don't remember the hugs or his scent. Surely, he did it in the birthing suite at Broward General Hospital. As he held me, he kissed me (that is what fathers do, right?). Dad kissed me on November 23, 1985, sometime after 6:45 in the morning. I'm almost certain. I don't remember that kiss, but I do remember the 9,999 kisses that never followed.

I will hide my tell-all-eyes from his see-all-eyes. They unveil my sins to my father. He hears my confession without repentance: I hate you.

***

Dad made me a prophetess, but I wanted to be a liar. "Mom this is a mistake! We should not drop our lives and follow him after a few weeks of good conversation. Did he encounter Christ on the road to Georgia? No. Therefore, he is the same lover whose fist tarred your eyes and stained your lips with your own blood, the father who abandoned his daughters and never called in nine years. As far as I'm concerned, he is a complete stranger. Mom, do you really think he has changed? What am I asking? Of course, he did; even maggots turn into flies and flies beget more maggots." If only I had the guts to share these sentiments with Mom...

***

"Mom, how did you meet my father?" I asked once again.

"Cheri, didn't I share this story with you before? I'm sure I did."

"I forgot." I told the truth. She scoffed and began. "I was twenty-five years old, and your Dad was twenty-six. We shared the same apartment building in Deerfield Beach, Florida. He lived in the apartment which faced the stairwell on the third floor. Your brother and I lived in a one bedroom on the same floor. At the time, I worked in the fields picking cotton to put food on the table. One day as I was climbing the stairs up to my apartment he introduced himself. He offered to help with my groceries while flirting with me. He was not my type."

“Why not?” I interrupted.

“I preferred more milk in my coffee. But, there is much to be said about persistence. I came home routinely after 5 p.m. and your father would position himself at the bottom of the stairwell like a guard. He earned my attention with his sweet smile and silly jokes. We began dating, fell in love, moved in together and every time he looked at me I was pregnant.” I smiled. “I felt like I won the jackpot when I met your father. He treated your brother as his own blood. He always wanted a son, and your brother needed a father.

“He worked like a mule to provide for us. Landscaping and tree cutting in Florida’s hot sun is not a joke. Yet, six days a week he left before sunrise and returned at sunset with grass-stained Dickies. I appreciated this about him. He also worked side jobs. Finally, we saved enough money to rent a house in Fort Lauderdale and then I was able to stop working and stay home with all of you. Your Dad always wanted to own his own business. I knew he would. He was extremely ambitious and intelligent. You get that from him.” I smiled again. “In less than a year he started purchasing landscaping equipment, and his dream came true.

“He was also generous. We helped many of our family members financially. We lost count of how many people we housed in their time of need. One of his cousins moved in and they became inseparable. He was instrumental in shaping the man you now know your father to be. It all started when he took your father to Isle Casino Racing Pompano Park. He taught him the ins and outs of horse racing and everything changed. Your father lost and won thousands of dollars in seconds. He developed a gambling problem which turned into an addiction. Your father began neglecting our family by choosing to spend his free time at the Casino. Some nights he did not return home. Other nights he returned plastered. His new lifestyle came with infidelity and to compensate for his insecurities he became abusive. Infidelity preceded physical abuse. To escape your father's wrath, I returned to work and tried keeping us afloat. Once his transformation was complete, the charming young man who won me over was a monster."

***

I watched Mom's hopes for a better life with a loving husband and caring father vaporize for the second time. Dad promised her everything she deserved, and more. Some things were spoken and others implied. "We will put our money together and buy a house. The girls deserve a house. I will get MacDana a computer. She needs one for homework. I will help you raise the girls. Daughters need their father. I am their father. I miss having my family. I've always loved you and I've never stopped. Let us forget everything that happened in the past and start over."

Granted, Dad was convincing. Even I swallowed a spoonful of his placebo while longing to be a Rudy Huxtable. Unfortunately, while we were apart, Dad never sought therapy for his gambling habits. He continued to be a womanizer. The women he settled with while Mom was away experienced his wrath. Mom left Dad nine years ago for all these reasons only to return to the same exact man, minus the beatings.

Secretly, I prayed for the beatings. I wanted him to hit her one more time so I could take vengeance for every woman who took a punch from Dad and scare straight every man like Dad. The beating would end with his head bleeding onto cold tiles with his eyes wide open. I would dial 911 with my bloody hand. Wait for the cops to clasp their cold handcuffs around my wrist. Plead guilty before a judge and spend the rest of my life humming to the sound of my father's blood streaming onto the tiles. Game over.

My *Braveheart* moment never materialized. He no longer abused Mom physically. Quite frankly, I think if Mom had a choice between a black eye or pacing the living room late at night waiting for his key to open the door; or walking into an empty apartment to find him sexing another woman; or crying in excruciating jealousy over the other woman; or paying all the bills after Dad had gambled and lost all his earnings; or learning of all the bastard children he had fathered. Mom would have happily chosen the black eye.

CHAPTER 8

CAPTIVITY HELD CAPTIVE

Number 15 flashed in red neon lights. Mom stared at her number 32 ticket and shook her head. We sat miserably at the Department of Motor Vehicle (DMV) because Mom needed a Sunshine State driver's license. We sat at the department and it was miserable. I had no choice in the matter. I was forced to come along for reasons only a mother could use. Just because she carried me for nine months and gave birth to me, she felt she had the right to drag me wherever and whenever she pleased.

The DMV reminded me of a black and white scene from The Twilight Zone. Everyone sat in the cold waiting area elbow-to elbow wearing faces that read, "I don't want to be here, but I don't have a choice." Their eyes obsessed over the digital queue displayed overhead. A toddler's whine turned into crying and then screaming, interrupting the low rumbling chatter in the room. A small T.V mounted high silently played the Maury show with captions speeding across the bottom of the screen. The room was winter cold. My naked arms were covered in goose bumps. I sighed, rolled my eyes, fidgeted until I could not take it any longer. "Mom, may I go outside, please? I'm freezing." She agreed. I walked outside into the summer air. It felt like soft warm sheets fresh out of the dryer. I wanted to declare like Martin L. King, "Free at last, free at last, thank God Almighty, I'm free at last." I skipped away from the building then leaped onto a yellow parking block, trying to keep my balance. I mastered my impromptu game within a few minutes. Boredom persisted, so I returned to a bench right outside the DMV door.

The door opened. A young man in his twenties bounced out with relief. Almost immediately he noticed me and smiled. I blushed. "Hello gorgeous, my name is Vegas. Do you have a name, beautiful, or can I just call you mine?" Attached to his boyish good looks was an exotic Jamaican accent. After I told him my name, he asked for my phone number. I didn't share it with him because my parents had strict rules against phone calls from strange older men, all boys, and all girls, except for my female church friends. In other words, the only man that could call my house looking for me was Jesus. Before heading to his car, he wrote his number on a piece of paper and made me promise to call him. As he drove away I slipped the paper into my bra and fantasized about him. Mom walked out the DMV with a smile identical to mine. She was the proud owner of a Florida Driver's License, and I had a secret tucked away in my bra.

Later that evening I waited impatiently for my parents to start snoring. The familiar sound finally arrived at 11:30. I snuck into the kitchen to call Vegas. "Hello, may I speak to Vegas please?" He was pleased I called.

"Hi gorgeous, *wah gwaan*?" I understood his first two words and the rest flew over my head. I giggled with excitement and confusion. Later, I learned *wah gwaan* meant "what's going on." We chatted briefly about what I was doing and what he was doing. He asked what I was wearing and complimented my voice, "You sound very sexy on the phone." Meanwhile, I was really trying to be quiet; careful not to stir my parents out of their sleep. My nerves were in overdrive. Mom or Dad could wake up at any time for a bathroom break and hear me on the phone. Vegas added to my uneasiness. I struggled to answer his successive questions while keeping an ear out for my parents. I didn't want to ruin my chance with him by giving a stupid answer. Several questions I answered with I-don't-know and others with simple one word answers.

"Beautiful, I really want to see you again."

"Ok"

"I'm coming to pick you up, tell me your address."

I never meant it was OK to see me again right now. I thought I was merely being agreeable. But I could not backtrack and risk sounding immature or timid. I gave him my address on Kathy Lane and my heart raced with fear and excitement. Should I change into something else and risk waking someone up? No, I could wear my pajamas. Perfect. How will I get out of this house without making a sound? The front door had a loud deadbolt, so that was out. The window near my dresser would have to do. Alright, step one: slide my radio over. Step two: step onto the dresser. Unlock the window. Pull the window up slowly. Stop. Listen for continued snoring from my parent's room.

"What are you doing," questioned my little sister.

"Shush, Nothing. Go back to sleep. I will be right back."

I opened the window wide enough to crawl through and then looked down and realized I'd forgotten my shoes. *Stupid, stupid, stupid!* Before I could think of going back inside, he pulled up to the curb with a two-door black Honda accord. I eased the window shut and ran to his car on two bare feet. I thought my heart would explode as we drove off. My mind started thinking of possibilities.

What if Mom woke up and spot-checked my room? What if this was a bad idea? I looked back towards the house, and the lights were still off. *Whew*!

"Are you ok?" Vegas interrupted. He caressed my knee. I snapped back to reality and took a deep breath. "Everything will be fine. Don't worry, beautiful." His words calmed my worries.

We arrived at his apartment after a short drive. He offered to carry me from the car to preserve my naked feet, but I decided to walk. He opened the door to his place and offered me something to drink, but I declined. I was too nervous. I glanced around as he told me to make myself at home. He turned on jazz and grabbed my hands. "Thank you for calling me, love. I was scared I would never see you again." I smiled and looked away. He led me into his bedroom; it was dark.

Moments later Vegas turned on the lights and allowed me to get dressed. I noticed the pictures on his dresser, but one woman's face was consistent. "Who is this?"

"My wife." He answered as he slipped into his shirt.

I thought, *did he just say his wife?!* "Where is she?"

"She is in Jamaica visiting family." Reality sunk in and so did shame.

"I'm ready to go home now," I whispered. He drove me home in silence. I walked away from his car without saying goodbye or looking back. When I got inside everyone was still asleep. I went to bed fully aware that at the age of fifteen, I'd just had my first one night stand.

Dear God,

I want to thank you for forgiving me time and time again. Your love is loyal. During the process of writing this manuscript, shame arose and took a seat in my heart. I know this is my past and you forgave it all. Thank you again. Seeing my story in black and white, it is clear to me spiritual warfare is real. The enemy wanted and still desires to steal my soul. He redirected my focus towards self-pleasure. Sex was all I wanted. It was my drug and my escape. My body was his vessel. I was the puppet, and he mastered all my strings. To see me ruined was not enough. He used me to destroy others. It was exhausting. Now, oh God, I look to you. Your yoke is easy and your burden is light.

God, allow your Holy conviction to enter the reader of my words. Pour your transformational anointing down like oil. Cancel the plan of self-destruction in this readers' life. Jesus Christ, I know you took captivity captive. Therefore, humiliation, shame, regret, and heartache must die. Let the Kingdom of God consume this book.

Jesus, let this reader be tired.

Amen

CHAPTER 9
TRAITOR

February 14, 2001, I walked into Coconut Creek High School and made my way through the noisy crowd of teens. As I approached my locker, the boy who stole my heart a month ago held my attention. Above his head swayed two-gigantic helium-filled balloons that read, "I Love You." In his arms, he cradled a heart-shaped box of chocolates and a gift bag. Excitement flushed my face, and my reaction was everything he'd hoped for. He attempted to hand it all over just as I wrapped my arms around him and kissed his cheek. "Thank you so, so much. I love it!"

"Open it," he instructed. I did and found a sparkling gift box of White Diamonds perfume widened my smile. "Keep looking, there is more."

"What? No way!"

Laughter overtook me as I unfolded a black novelty t-shirt. We embraced again. I wanted to hug him forever, but the first school bell rang. My cheeks ached as I walked away from my first valentine. In less than nine months I would be sixteen, yet, if my parents knew I had a boyfriend…I would be homeschooled in Haiti. Meanwhile, "xoxo" defaced the girl's bathroom and couples were sucking each other's face off in the hallways. Public displays of affection never sat well with me, but attention from a guy gave me life. My false sense of identity was established in the opposite sex.

What happens at school stays at school, right? He was my boyfriend Monday through Friday within Creek's walls. The chances of my parents discovering I had a boyfriend were slim to none. I was the proud girlfriend of an upper-classman. He was a senior and I a sophomore. We met in the choir room when Creek's band and choir collaborated for Christmas. He walked around school with drumsticks tucked into his backpack, always ready for an impromptu performance. He kept to himself outside of the band room but transformed on the field while marching with his drum line. I liked him simply because he liked me. And, did I mention he was a boy?

I spent the remaining school day in a euphoric daze, toting my balloons around school. My sense of self-worth attached to inanimate objects. So many of us paraded around with our ostentatious gifts, loudly but silently proclaiming, "Someone loves me…just look at my presents."

The final school bell rang. Valentine's Day was over. As I walked towards the school buses I released my balloons to the wind. It felt awful, but it would have been preposterous to try and sneak them home past my parents. I tossed the gift bag into a trash bin before boarding the bus. On the ride home, I hid my two remaining gifts at the bottom of my backpack, hoping to beat my parents home from work.

Mom won. Her car parked in its parking space was a huge disappointment. I unlocked the front door, saluted Mom and sealed it with a kiss on her cheek as she prepared dinner. I felt like Judas before I turned away and she stopped me with, "*Kè ou se kè kontan jodi a*, your heart is a happy heart today." As if when I turned away the fletching from cupids arrow stuck out my back. *Was she fishing,* I thought. "Who was your Valentine?" My heart dropped, *can she see through my backpack?* "Don't lie to your mother. You can tell me the truth, boo-boo." *Why did she have to say boo-boo?* Suddenly, she turned into the coolest mom ever. I melted into her with frenzy as I unzipped my backpack. After years of praying for a healthy mother-daughter relationship, a door cracked open. I wanted to tell her everything. How we met and all the admirable things about him. I needed her guidance about dating and falling in love. Who knew she cared? She abandoned the kitchen and sat with me at our dining room table. She regarded the bottle, splashed my perfume on her wrist, rubbed, aired, and sniffed. We gushed together. "Oh, this young man has great taste. Is he your boyfriend? You can tell me." I nodded yes. Before I could tell her about his cute curls, keys rattled at the front door.

I froze and stared at the rotating doorknob in disbelief. Dad was home earlier than usual. Mom, equally stunned, ceased talking and smiling. As he walked over to set his lunch box down I grew afraid, my insides felt like bricks. I walked over to greet him with a kiss. My heart pounded loudly in betrayal. "What is this?" He pointed at my gift.

"Oh…um one of my girl-friends at school gave them to me." My tongue had a mind of its own. A dumb one.

"Is that right? A girl gave this to you?" He smiled, but it didn't reach his eyes. It was a poorly constructed lie I never planned to utter. I panicked. Dad normally came home after sunset. Why did Mom stop me? SLAP!

A steady piercing sound rang in my ear. I blinked in shock and disbelief. I never saw the second hit coming. SLAP! The weight of his hand across my face felt like a cement brick. My body collapsed onto the tiles. He exploded into rage. My mind crashed. I felt helpless. He grabbed my shirt by its collar and dragged me across the room. I screamed in absolute fear for my life. I kicked like a wild animal and reached for Mom but she just stood there. I reached for the wall. My hands slipped. "MOM! HELP ME, PLEASE HELP ME!" She did not move. He flung me into my room. I slid away as fast as I could to my dresser. My shirt was torn open and my bra exposed.

Dad stared at me in silent rage and disgust. I sobbed and noticed my little sister on the top bunk crying for me. Mom walked in with a new attitude. "You deserve it," she said. "We sent you to school to get an education. But instead, like the disobedient pile of crap you are, you go get a boyfriend. And you have been lying to our faces. Oh yeah, you deserve it." She yanked my radio from the wall. "It's all this damn love music." SMASH. She smashed the radio to the ground and its pieces went flying. Mom fooled me twice. Shame on me. Tears streamed down my face, but I was done crying.

Mom made me clean up her mess. White Diamonds never touched my skin until this very day. Everything went into the dumpster.

The traitor entered my room before going to bed and said, "You are staying home from school tomorrow!"

"Yes Mom," I lied again.

Everyone fell asleep, and I stared at the ceiling. Sleeping was out of the question: midway into the evening I got dressed. My face throbbed when I bent over to lace my sneakers. I slipped out of the window and started walking. Four miles later, I stood in front of Creek High. It was empty and locked. I sat on a bench and fell asleep. The clicking sound of shoes bolted me awake. Creek opened; I held my head high with a pounding headache and walked past the stares of the administrative staff in the main office. A school counselor's door was open and I entered without knocking. She tried, but failed, to contain her reaction. "Who did that to you?"

"My Dad."

I documented the sequence of events which led to my black eye and the bruise around my neck. Two officers arrived and escorted me home. Mom opened the door in disbelief. They asked to speak with Dad, coincidently, he never returned home from work. He reappeared a week later.

CHAPTER 10
CONFESSIONS

"MacDana is having sex," declared Dad.

"No, she is not," Mom argued. "My daughter is a virgin. She is only sixteen... of course she's a virgin." She tried to convince herself.

"Ask her."

Please don't ask me. Please don't ask me, I prayed.

"MacDana, are you a virgin?" Mom's intimidating glare did not work. I was taught to never look an adult in the eye.

"Yes, Mom," I continued to stare at the tiles on the ground.

"If you are lying to me, I will find out." Her voice grew louder. "One visit to the doctor and I will have the truth. This is your last chance to tell me the truth. Are you still a virgin?"

"Yes, Mom."

She rolled her eyes at Dad.

"Woman, it is obvious she is having sex... just look at her neck," said Dad. As they quarreled, I snuck into the bathroom. I could still hear them in the kitchen. "Thank you God, thank you God, thank you God," I whispered. *How did Dad know? My neck?*

What about my neck gave my secrets away? I don't have a hickey. I was confused.

But he was right. I was having SO much sex, I could barely remember all their names. There were a few men in GA, one of which would have been guilty of sleeping with a minor. When we moved back to Florida, stress increased my sexual drive. Next door to our apartment lived four brothers under the age of thirty. As soon as Mom and Dad went to work during the summer I wore my shorts, shorter and my shirts tighter to take the trash out. It worked! There was another man who lived across the street. We met at Publix Supermarket and several days later I sat naked on his bed. Not to mention the one night stand. When school started, finding trouble was easy. Boys were everywhere. This football player, that football player. Boys, boys, and more boys.

Dad is right, and Mom is in denial. She knows I am not a virgin, I told the woman in the mirror. *The doctor told her so when I was a little girl. Maybe she never shared our family secret with Dad. Either way, Mom is a liar too.*

***

She frightened me in the middle of the night. "Open your legs." She didn't wait for me to obey, she opened them herself. She searched for evidence of penetration. I thought of pulling away, but how? She would assume I was guilty as sin. She continued to search. Humiliation mixed with horror rendered me powerless. A thick line was crossed. "It is customary in Haiti for a mother who suspects her daughter of being sexually active to conduct a vaginal inspection. And if she is positive for penetration, she is punished with the application of either a scotch bonnet pepper or freshly squeezed lime juice in her vagina," said Mom. The key word was Haiti. In America, it is called: child abuse.

I prayed until she finished. She exited my room satisfied. Me, mortified.

CHAPTER 11
THE DROUGHT

I couldn't hold it any longer. Streams of urine were seconds from running down my legs. Window shopping and petty theft enthralled me until my bladder was too full to ignore. I began speed walking at Coral Square Mall towards the ladies' room. A few more steps down a long corridor and...

"Hi!" he startled me.

"Hi," I responded as I continued to move past him. I made it to the restroom and thankfully a stall was open. I washed my hands and took a quick look in the mirror before returning to Macy's.

"Hi!" It was him again. He was proud of himself. The grin on his face boasted that he'd done something special. I stopped and conversed for a few minutes. Towards the end of our flirtatious exchange he handed me a prewritten-torn strip of paper with his contact information. He was presumptuous. He was right. I blushed and stuffed it in my pocket.

I almost forgot about him, but the paper tumbled onto the ground as I sorted dirty clothes. My lack of interest in him was odd. I never had a type or a look which appealed to me. Regarding the opposite sex, I was an equal opportunist. However, something about him raised questions I could not make sense of. Yet, boredom was explicit; I called him to bring it to an end and that he did. He was an expert storyteller. The greatest story he ever told me started like this, "My name is Shaquan. I'm currently home on military leave."

"The military?" I was impressed.

"Oh yeah, I guess I forgot to tell you, I'm a soldier in the United States Army."

"That is so cool! What is it like? Did you ever shoot anyone?"

"I'm not allowed to talk about that."

"Oh." *Grow up MacDana,* "Sorry."

"I wish I could tell you more, but I'm sworn to secrecy."

"Wow."

"But I was in Iraq."

"Oh my God. How long have you been in the military?"

"A little over a year."

"How old are you?"

"I'm nineteen." He shared a few war stories that could have been a good movie and I later discovered parts of them were. The other parts belonged to people he knew. Two of his brothers served in the military. One was a marine and the other a soldier. His close friend was also a marine. He, on the other hand, had difficulty passing the standardized entrance exam for the military. Being in the military was only one lie, tied into countless others. Shaquan was his alias. Lastly, he was not nineteen, he was twenty-two. Truths surfaced long after I fell head over heels in "lust," and called it "love."

***

"I love you," I declared.

"I love you," he said.

Love or lust? Two four-lettered words. They both begin with "L" yet, are grossly different; like life and death. Masked-lust will declare a secret war against its owner. The owner rises higher and higher on waves of empty promises. When the disguise comes off, the crash is thunderous as lust reveals its carnality. I thought I saw an ocean in the distance with tunnel vision. I never tasted salt in the wind. I never felt the wind riding the ocean. I drew closer and saw the bland truth I tasted. There was never an ocean of love. It was nothing more than a shallow lagoon of lust.

I never knew him to love him. Meanwhile, night after night I sinned against myself in his car, and in his bed. Infatuation peaked, while good judgment and caution faded.

"You whore! You are the mother of whores. I had to hear it from the neighbors. How embarrassing! While we were sleeping, you've been sneaking out our window to meet a guy in a black car," said Mom.

"He is my boyfriend!" SLAP. *I knew that was coming.*

"That is not your boyfriend, you fool! That is a *vagabond* having a good time in your vagina. A good man knocks on the door at a decent hour and meets your family. He does not ask you to dishonor yourself and your family and sneak around at night. He only wants what is in between your legs."

"If that is your boyfriend," said Dad, "Invite him to the house."

***

"My parents want to meet you. Can you come over on Friday at 6?"

"What are you talking about? I don't want to meet your parents."

"But you are my boyfriend, and you said you loved me. This is what boyfriends do."

"Do you want me to go to jail?!"

"Of course, not. Why would you go to jail?"

"You are sixteen and I am really twenty-two. I can go to jail for statutory rape."

"What! You lied to me? Why would you lie to me? Whatever, it doesn't matter now. My parents just want to meet you. You have to come."

"Let me check my schedule."

"I need you to be here on Friday at 6pm. Ok?"

"Ok."

He didn't show up and the phone never rang. Dad left at 7:30. He refused to look at me. Mom rubbed it in. I called, but he didn't answer. Days passed and finally we reconnected. "Who does that?" I asked. "Why didn't you show up for me? We waited close to an hour for you. You embarrassed me, but you said you loved me." I broke down in tears. He continued to listen in silence. "The least you could have done was call me or at least answer my calls."

***

Baby sister was sandwiched between Mom and I in the church pew. Prayer meeting started at 7 p.m. but we walked in late, so we sat in the rear. The church was the last place I cared to be. Tension and anger decorated our home. Mom became plagued with Tourette's Syndrome, triggered by my presence. Her words cut into me like a whip. With each slash, my inner being ripped apart. My boyfriend abandoned ship. I called him like a stalker, but he ignored each attempt to reach him. My world was spinning wildly; I could not process this heartbreak. I was overwhelmed with emotions.

Mom stood and proceeded to walk towards the podium. "*Beni soit L'eternel, beni soit L'eternel, beni soit L'eternel.*" I watched with fear as she shouted bless the Lord while she adjusted the microphone. The congregation responded. What is she doing? I thought.

"My brothers and sisters, I stand here tonight with a special prayer request." Her voice quivered. "Please, help me pray for my daughter MacDana." *Excuse me!* "Our neighbors recently informed me she has been sneaking out of her window at night and meeting with a strange man to have sex in his car." She wept.

What in the hell just happened? Everyone turned around to take a good look at Jezebel reincarnated. *Stop looking at me. Face forward and get out of my face!*

"Oh, mon Dieu!" said the usher as she turned to me. *Oh, my God*, was all I could think, as well. Mom's public announcement severed the thin string holding us together. In a church full of people (including a few of my classmates) she exposed my sins. Several people shook their heads in disappointment. Embarrassment gripped me. I wanted to crawl under a pew with a church blanket

and cover myself until the service ended. Suddenly, embarrassment birthed anger. *All of you can go to hell.* I grabbed my purse, took one last look at the traitorous fool crying into the mic, and exited the sanctuary.

I tried calling my boyfriend once again from a pay phone. He answered. Moments later we drove away from the church. He wanted sex, and I needed an escape. Several hours later I returned to the last place I wanted to be, home. Mom and Dad welcomed me.

"I want you out of my house, you nasty piece of shit," said Mom, the faithful church attendee. Dad empowered her with his presence.

"Ok." I walked past them towards my room and prayed mom wouldn't strike me again. Instead, she followed me to my room. "Don't touch anything in this house that I purchased. I bought your clothes." I shrugged and grabbed my school books and stuffed them into my backpack. "Sluts don't need books. You will never be anything more than a slut. You won't graduate. YOU ARE NOTHING! After everything I sacrificed for you, this is what you have become." She started crying. "I suffered so much to give you a better life." Her words drowned in her tears. "This is how you repay me. If they told me you would do this to me MacDana, I would have called them a liar. You piece of shit. I'm finished with you." I noticed baby sister on her top bunk fighting tears. I made it easy on her and left without a word or a second look.

As I stood curbside awaiting my boyfriend to rescue me, a patrol car slowed to a stop in front of me. Two officers walked towards me. I didn't know what to say or do. They began to question me, and I realized my parents had called them. Mom and Dad walked outside, and one of the officers broke away to talk to them. Finally, they explained to my parents I was free to leave if that was what I wanted.

I wanted to say, *Officer, I'd rather rot in jail then endure one more day in that loveless home. I don't have a plan or a place to go, but I am certain the unknown is better than the known. I'm tired of being slapped in the face and called out of my name. I feel less than, and I can't bear anymore. If this is life, take me out of misery with the gun in your holster.*

Mom sobbed like a child as she followed Dad back into the house. I remained outside waiting for him to arrive. Finally, he did.

CHAPTER 12
GAMBLER

My boyfriend wasn't interested in sharing his space. As other teenagers settled into their beds, I tried to get comfortable at an empty bus stop. My book bag doubled as a pillow, and I placed my feet on the bench. The temperature dropped a few degrees so I hugged myself for warmth. Sleep stole me away for an hour, but fear startled me awake again. I sat straight up and started counting cars to stay alert. Finally, daylight broke and the city bus parted its doors in front of my bus stop. I entered without fare, but the bus driver responded with a free, ride-all-day pass. I arrived at school with yesterday's clothes and rushed to the girls' bathroom. With wet brown paper towels and hand soap, I freshened up. I tossed my old underwear into the trash and pushed it to the bottom of the bin. After finger-combing my hair into a messy ponytail, I made my way to class.

The sound of the lunch bell at 11:00 a.m. caused my mouth to water. This was the first time school lunch excited me. Nothing went to waste on my lunch tray. I stowed leftovers in my backpack for dinner. After lunch, I fell asleep in class against my will. The classroom was empty when my instructor tapped me awake. "Dear, is everything alright at home? It's not like you to sleep during my class." I ignored her question with an apology as I hurried towards the door. I didn't feel like sobbing.

Most nights I wandered the streets until my feet ached. I preferred bus stops because they were lit. As I began to settle down for the night, two officers startled me. After a brief Q&A, they drove me to an all-girls shelter in Fort Lauderdale Beach. A weary, middle-aged woman greeted me with the best smile one could give at 0' dark thirty in the morning. She wasted no time before escorting me down a corridor and into a room. The room was furnished with two bunk beds, two desks, and two chairs. Two of the beds were occupied, and one of the girls turned away from the outside light while covering her head with a blanket. "We will fully register you in the morning. But tonight, get some rest." She shut the door behind her, and I went straight to the bottom bunk. I slept into the morning. When I finally awoke, my roommates were gone, but a welcome kit was left on my bed. It included a toothbrush with toothpaste, soap, sanitary napkins, a washcloth, and towel. I cleaned up and went to the front office. There was a long list of rules and a curfew which required my signature. "Are you hungry, child?" asked a different woman than the one from the night before.

"Starving!" I replied. She decided a tour was in order first. I was relieved it ended at the dining hall. After washing down my sandwich with a Capri sun, I ventured into the lobby and sat alone. There were girls of different ages and races socializing there. Each one had a story fit for a good book. The pregnant girls made me extremely uncomfortable. I could hear my parents, "It's only a matter of time before you are pregnant and useless. You will never amount to anything." I wanted to run away from them as if pregnancy was contagious. *The cursed words of my parents will not produce fruit. I will not be pregnant and useless.* After two nights there, I left and never returned.

Walking alone on State Road 7 after school became my favorite past time. Cars with places to go hurried up and down; I felt safe in the traffic. As rush hour ended a car slowed down next to me. The driver was a black male who appeared to have stuffed himself into the vehicle. He crouched over the steering wheel to avoid the ceiling and his muffin top spilled onto his center console. "Young lady, do you need a ride?" I hesitated and said no. "Are you sure? It's hot out here and I don't mind giving you a ride." There was comfort in his baritone voice which convinced me after I said no. I did not have a place to call home, but I was tired of being alone and on the streets.

As we drove I told him the truth, the only place I had to go was to school in the morning. In return, he offered me a room in his house. I had nothing left to lose except my life. I gambled and trusted him with it. He was over fifty, a tall, hefty man who towered above me. He had a slow gait due to a bad leg or foot. He did not talk much, and his temperate personality reminded me of a friendly giant. I followed him out of his car towards a one-story home with peeling paint. The lawn was sprinkled with trash and patches of dead grass. Outside the home matched the inside. We walked through a dark and cluttered living room. Behind the front door were shelves filled with snacks and candy which he sold to the neighbors. I continued to follow him further into his home.

We stopped in front of a door and he shoved it open. A cluttered bedroom, including an old waterbed, was being used as storage for his dead mother's belongings. "You can sleep in here as long as you'd like. The bathroom is right across the hall. Come and go as you please, but don't bring anyone over. Is that understood?"

"Yes," I said, "Thank you."

I had my very own room again. The waterbed's novelty quickly grew old, but it was far better than a bus bench. We barely interacted with each other. He only engaged me to ask a courteous, "How goes it?" At night, he drank like a sailor in the living room. He illuminated it with a disco ball and played very loud music. His friends and patrons stopped by at odd hours to join him or buy numbers. He studied numerology and over time the locals renamed him "The Numbers Man." They paid him to interpret numbers seen in dreams, but mainly they wanted the next winning lottery ticket. Business was steady. I mentioned my living arrangements to the only friend in school I trusted. She knew exactly who he was and said, "…that ain't all he's sellin.' We gotta get you outta there. Come live with me!"

She lived in a small two-bedroom apartment located in the rough side of Pompano Beach, FL. Her apartment barely fit her family, yet she welcomed me with ease. Her mom cooked, and we ate together. She braided extensions into my hair so I wouldn't have to worry about my appearance. I shared her clothes and her favorite vanilla body splash by Victoria's Secret. We walked to school together and became best friends, more like sisters. I appreciated the sense of belonging she offered me.

The pangs of homelessness are not limited to lack of shelter; I felt like a wolf without her pack. God sent strangers and friends along my journey to house me, feed me, dress me and love me when I could not love myself. It is important to look back at the road traveled or you will overlook the other footprints in the sand. Grace and mercy covered me during this time of my life. To the bus driver who donated the bus pass to me without speaking a word: thank you from the bottom of my heart. To the strange man who gave me my own room in his home; thank you so very much. You blessed me and may blessings return unto you without measure. Many people go missing and are never found again. Some are dead while others are sold into sex-trafficking, but God protected me. I walked out of his home in one piece. There were many other angels disguised as strangers and good Samaritans. Thank you with kisses. As for my school friend and her family who offered me a place to call home; it is impossible to repay you with a gift that embodies my gratitude. May your days be filled with joy and may God always provide for your family.

THIRD TIME'S THE CHARM

My friend and her family were forced to move out of state. They invited me to come with them but I wanted to finish my senior year and attend graduation. I stayed behind in Pompano with no place to call home. I attempted to sleep in their empty apartment, but…

The roaches were fighting me for the crumbs; the rats were fighting me for the cheese, and the demons fought for my soul. Right next door lived her so-called "uncle" who gave us the creeps. I only greeted him because Mom raised me to respect my elders. He lived in a shotgun apartment. From the door, you could see the entire unit. He managed to squeeze everything he needed into the tiny space, including a viciously trained Rottweiler. She remained chained, but under the right circumstance, the chain would easily break.

He invited me to stay with him until something better came along, and I accepted from a place of desperation. I stood taller than him, but what he lacked in height he compensated with bulky muscles. I wondered if he and the dog were having a muscle competition. At sixty-five years old, he dressed in white tank tops and sweatpants. His head appeared oversized, like a four-month-old baby minus the cuteness.

The enemy uses the same weapon to attack. Rape followed me and every few years it reared its ugly head. At first, I didn't identify this next life event as rape.

My second night there he unchained the dog as he walked into the apartment and announced I couldn't stay with him for free. In so little words he said I had to have sex with him in exchange for a place to sleep. I don't remember how or when he forced himself inside me. I laid on my back on his full-sized bed and cried somewhere so deep within, tears never surfaced. As my soul wept, I hurried and buried every minute of the moment somewhere in my mind where I kept my "never happened" memories. I didn't want to remember his scent, his touch, his face or his name. A fear of not forgetting drove me to work overtime. I didn't want to live with this filth in my head. I could not cope. It had enough power to damage me for life.

I never screamed for help nor did I beg or ask him to stop. It seemed pointless at the time. He made his position clear when he used the dog as reinforcement. I crumbled on the inside as he satisfied his loins. I rolled over when he finished and stared at the wall for hours. Before sunlight broke, I packed my bags and never saw him again.

Before writing this book, I never mentioned this to a single soul. As hard as I tried to erase the memory, it didn't work. Instead, I felt tainted because of the sordid details. I did not consider it rape because of my inaction. I concluded that...

The girl needed a place to sleep.

The man had a place for the girl to sleep.

The man wanted sex as payment.

The girl had a vagina.

The man got paid in full.

However, let's set all politics aside and evaluate this scene in its entirety. I never expressed any love interest for this guy. My hips didn't move under him with desire. My lips never kissed him, and my eyes did not search to connect with his in the act. If that weight-lifting midget and his dumb dog hadn't scared me, touching me would not have been an option.

Instead, it would have been a scene from a Quentin Tarantino movie. After he and his dog made their demands, in slow motion, I would have levitated off the bed like a praying mantis and, with the heel of my good foot, rearranged his jaw. And as for the bitch in the room, I dare you to bark at me again.

***

One night I met a strange woman who said, "You are a beautiful young woman. I would give anything to look like you again. These men should be eating out of your hands. Don't be a fool and give it away for free. They must pay to play. Remember that! Nothing is free in America, especially not that thing in between your legs."

Around sunset a white, two-door Ford F150 drove east on Coconut Creek Parkway. Nostalgia hit me as my eyes followed the vehicle. It looked much like my Dad's truck. I missed my sister and my mom, but mostly my sister. I missed our late-night chats. Halfway down the road the driver made a U-turn and, as he approached me, he slowed down. My dad stared at me, laughing hysterically. Apparently, the sight of me standing on the side of the road without a home to call my own amused him. He pointed at me in mockery before driving away. I lost sight of his truck, but I continued to hear his inappropriate laughter swirling around me. It drowned my thoughts and the sound of cars passing by. The cacophony played in a deafening loop, awaiting my defeat.

Mid-evening, a black four-door Ford F450 drove east on Coconut Creek Parkway. My Dad's laughter continued as the truck made a U-turn and stopped in front of me. Dark-tinted windows rolled down and a strange man said, "Would you like a ride?" I desperately needed a distraction, so I reached for the door handle in acceptance. He drove to a nearby motel. Moments later I stood naked in the dingy room. He was pleasantly surprised with my lack of inhibition, my numbness. He was built like a linebacker and covered in tattoos. Nothing about him was pleasant. He could have crushed me with one hand.

Even so, he was unable to scare the hurt out of me. What was so funny to my Dad, I wondered? My despondency! He drove past me to ridicule me. His daughter. I stood still before the stranger who called himself Buck, awaiting love, but settle for being the butt of another man's joke. Buck had his way with me until I seized with physical pain. Yet, nothing he did could lessen the constant evisceration of my soul.

Before he went off to his other life, and without solicitation, he left some money on the nightstand. I stared at my payment with repugnance and defeat. Dad's laughter suddenly stopped when I realized I had enough money to make it through another week.

I found a creative way to survive with pain; it's called selective amnesia. After years of rape after rape, I taught myself how to forget distressing memories, temporarily.

Truth is: I never forgot, but I did bury them. The grass grew tall enough for me to pretend it never happened. But under the dirt, forever remained my story. When rape happens to, let's say a woman, unwanted miles are obviously placed on her, but that is the least of her problems. She is hemorrhaging in the spirit. Tracking blood everywhere, fading.

Many of you walk around witnessing people bleed to death, and your reactions break God's heart. Some of you lash out judgments with your words and your stares. "What in the world is she wearing? Slut! What!? She slept with how many guys?! Hoe, hoe, hoe!" The worst people are the men who see it as an opportunity to add another score to their conquest-board. Men, listen! If a woman allows you to have your way with her body and you know you are not her husband and you didn't earn those privileges, she is most likely wounded and dying right in front of you. This is an excellent opportunity to practice the definition of a real man. Take some time to inquire and get to know her history. Need a reason? Imagine your sister in a precarious situation like this. What would you want the man to say to her?

As for me, being raped as a toddler opened the door for every sexual struggle I indulged in. Many children are still being exploited, abused, raped, and violated. Parents, don't forget to pray and talk to your little ones. Most people believe Sunday prayers recited in unison with the congregation are enough. BUT THAT IS NOT ENOUGH! These weekly prayers won't stand a chance against the predators of the spirit. Pray without ceasing.

Throughout the years, guilt and shame anchored me to these terrible memories. I felt guilty without reason. Guilt is sneaky like that, attaching itself to nothing. My shame grew when I compared myself to women who I thought were blessed. "Why not me God?" My eyes were out of focus. I could not see Jesus Christ who nailed it all to the cross.

CHAPTER 13

HAVE YOU SEEN MY BABIES?

Have you ever seen 'The Walking Dead'? It is a post-apocalyptic television series. The entire show revolves around zombies feeding on people. During its first season, the Jones family was introduced: Morgan Jones, Jenny Jones, and Duane Jones. Jenny, a walking dead, lurked outside the home her son and husband barricaded themselves in. One night Morgan ventured into the basement without his son. Several minutes later, he returned to find Jenny making her way towards Duane. Before Morgan could save Duane, Jenny took a chunk out of their only son as he screamed for his life. She satisfied her sole desire; to feed her flesh.

An old friend analogized, "Most people are like zombies. They sometimes lack a real thought or emotion. They have no awareness of self, others, or God. It is called ZOMBIE MODE!"

I was once a zombie too.

***

At seventeen years old, I decided to move from my friends family's house and in with a guy I was sleeping with. I started working as a cashier at K-mart as I figured out what I was going to do now that high school was over. I assumed he was my boyfriend. To my knowledge, we were in an exclusive relationship. Our status, however, did not curb his appetite for other women. I cried, we fought, he apologized, I accepted, and several weeks later he did it again. To my detriment, I desperately wanted someone to call my own. I stopped at nothing to earn his love. I tried to get to his heart through his stomach, but failed. I cleaned his room and washed his clothes, but he did not need a second mom. I attempted to buy his love, but I could not afford it. I idolized and made him my god; it went unnoticed.

To screen my blighted reality I turned to alcohol. Inebriation spun me to sleep when words like desperate and pathetic taunted me. So, like any pitiful woman, I accepted the nothings he gave me. He gave me his sex, and at that moment, he sometimes glanced at me. It numbed my afflicted heart for less than thirty minutes a day. My loins tried to convince my heart it was real love, but the heart is no fool.

Then one morning the strangest set of events happened at my job at K-mart. A woman paused at the cash register and stared at me. She ended the awkwardness and asked, "Are you feeling okay, Ma'am?" Before I could respond with a lie, I passed out. Several people rushed to my side. After I regained consciousness and got to my feet, the strange woman ushered me to a seat. "How are you feeling now?" She probed.

"I think I'm hungry. I didn't have breakfast this morning." All I could think about was food.

"Are you pregnant?" I shook my head no. "Are you sure?"

She encouraged me to take a pregnancy test. I did and discovered the truth. We were expecting a baby.

I thought our relationship would finally take a turn down

lover's lane. I imagined his heart for me when I shared the news. Instantly, love would steer him to righteousness, and the baby and I would be the source of his affection and devotion. No more arguing and infidelity. The magical baby which grew within me would change everything: love, marriage, then a baby carriage. My thoughts ran away from common sense until I shared with him, "I'm pregnant. Actually, we are pregnant."

He did not say much at first. He never looked at me or my flat stomach. "What do you want to do?" he asked. I shrugged my shoulders. I wanted him to say let's get ready to have a baby. But instead, he offered to pay for an abortion. I agreed, after listening to reasons why aborting was the right thing to do for us, for him. I convinced myself a reward awaited my sacrifice; a title, perhaps "the ultimate ride or die chick," or real love. I grasped at straws to press pass what was to come. I would forever remember at seventeen years old, I stood for nothing.

ZOMBIE MODE! *Wanting to feel loved by a man ruled everything about me. Like a leaf in the wind, my dreams, morals, and self-identity drifted in every direction. The man made it obvious he did not love me, but sex anchored me to this quicksand. I reduced myself to nothing. A dead man stands for nothing and falls for everything. My Christian upbringing said thou shall not murder. But zombies don't keep commandments. Death begets death. I responded to lust and the fear of not being loved. Just like the dead mother who ate her only begotten son. How can I value a gift when I don't value myself?*

We arose early to make it to the clinic by 8:30 am. I did not know what to expect. My mind was completely void of emotions like fear, joy, or anything appropriate. He drove me to a plaza on

State Rd. 7. I remembered strolling past it before and never noticed it was an abortion clinic. He drove to the front door and stopped. "Ummm, call me when you're done," he said.

"What? You are not coming inside with me? I have to do this on my own?" I realized he'd already made up his mind so I ended my protest by exiting his car. I walked toward the clinic. *This is it... there's no going back now.* A cold wind ushered me into an empty lobby. A woman slid a glass window open as I approached. She asked me to sign in and confirmed my appointment. I paid her with cash. She asked if I wanted anesthesia for an extra fee, but I could not cover the cost. She dismissed me with paperwork. I filled in the highlighted areas and minutes later another woman escorted me to the back.

We entered an exam room and she gave me a hospital gown to change into. Before she left me alone, she reminded me to remove my panties. I did as she instructed and sat down as the hairs on my arms stood straight up. I was freezing, but I distracted myself with posters on the wall. The woman reentered with another woman wearing a white coat.

I struggled to recollect the details of this day. It's lost in my history of "Things I Wish I Never Did." Yet I know the gist of it due to my work as a surgical technologist.

I placed my feet into stirrups and allowed my legs to fall open. The doctor exposed my cervix with a speculum and then grabbed it with a tenaculum. Dilators prepped my cervix for a suction curette. Once the curette was in place (next to our baby), she flipped the switch on. The loud vacuum sucked the life out of me.

My blood gushed into that dumb canister. My future clung to the wall of that cheap canister. My baby cried from inside that stupid canister. My baby was buried in that miserable canister. A piece of me died in that pathetic canister.

ROUND TWO

We met on the dance floor at the Palladium nightclub. He asked for a dance and I accepted. When the song ended, he held my hand and asked for another. He was enchanting, and his salsa was effortless. After many nights dipping and turning on the dance floor, we decided to date seriously. A couple months later I moved in with him and veils fell off. Small arguments ensued. "Why do you have to go dancing all the time… Let's do something different for once. Fine, go without me. Oh, so you're really going without me? Just, go!" I renamed him Happy Feet as I grew jealous of his hobby. I tried to control him with ultimatums, "dancing, or me?" It pushed him further away. Then one day he started to pick up on how irrational I'd been acting and paused to ask, "How long have you been pregnant?"

I had no idea our baby sat in my womb, to say nothing of how long. We confirmed his statement and hope revisited our struggling relationship. "We have a child on the way, *mi vida*. Let's make us work." He was excited about our future offspring. He wanted a daughter with curly hair. He was Mexican with Catholic upbringing. My thoughts of abortion never crossed his mind; it offended his religion. He cried with joy. Meanwhile, I cried with ambivalence. I did not feel we were in a position to bring a child into our world. We disagreed about so much. Our finances were tight because I was in-between jobs and taking classes at a community college. Perhaps if I were in love; but the truth was, I had one foot out the door. I was indecisive.

As the baby grew within me, chronic pelvic pain plagued me. At night, I twisted and turned to find relief, to no avail. The obstetrician said, "… pain often accompanies pregnancy" and dismissed me with over-the-counter pain relievers. None of which worked, by the way. My boyfriend tried to comfort me, he rubbed my back, but nothing helped. I felt alone in the world and trapped in my body during this time. Some nights my boyfriend would escape to a club and leave me alone. He could not stand being helpless as I suffered from pain night after night. I did not want to be pregnant, and the pain reinforced my stance on the matter.

One night I tried to pray away my living nightmare, but fell asleep and entered another. I had no idea I was dreaming. Everything was exactly the same: my room, my pajamas, even the T.V. was still on. Then I noticed a tiny naked fetus asleep in the palm of my right hand. I carried the baby into the kitchen and sat it on the blades of an empty blender. Before returning to bed, I turned on the stovetop and placed the blender in the center of the stove. I awoke from the dream screaming and sobbing. "The baby is going to die!"

"It's just a bad dream, *Mi Amor*. Everything will be fine," he said. He assured himself.

Several days later he decided some fresh air would do me good. We headed to the park for a game of soccer. My complete disregard for life started when I decided to run after the ball at full speed. I even stopped to do a few cartwheels mid stride. My boyfriend asked if I felt ok and I said yes while tackling him to the ground. He cautioned me to take it easy with concern for our unborn child. But I blew him off with another tackle and laughed out loud. Apathy became my adrenaline. I left the playground satisfied with my efforts. That baby did not stand a chance.

The following Monday my boyfriend and I followed a technician into a room for an ultrasound. It was time to hear our baby's heartbeat for the first time. He cocooned my right hand into his as we watched the technician's face during my exam. His excitement spilled onto me as I waited to hear the rapid thuds of our baby's heart. Something about the exam caused the technician to raise a brow and request my doctor's presence. My doctor explained to us that many first-time pregnancies ended with a miscarriage. I misled everyone and concealed my first pregnancy. The lie ensnared me. Finally, she encouraged us with stories that started like ours and ended with a newborn. I held his hand as we walked to the car. Before starting the engine, he held his face and sobbed. I felt ashamed and sorry for his loss.

After surgically removing the fetus from my womb, I went to the pharmacy with an oxycodone prescription for cramps. The cramps felt like a normal menstrual cycle, but I took the pills anyway. Despair, regret, and hopelessness overwhelmed me. I curled into a fetal position and mourned like a mother who lost her child. I had no desire to become a mom quite yet, but what I thought would be a relief taught me that physical pain hurts less than heartache. I took three pills a day for sedation. I wanted to sleep forever, or until the woman I had become disappeared. When oxy melted into my bloodstream, anxiety over my ending relationship faded and my guilt over the day at the park which ended our baby's life vanished.

I lived with my choice as best I could. I knew women who would do anything to have a baby, yet were unable to conceive. I felt guilty about my choice in their world. Sometimes I watched with regret as a child wrapped small arms around their mother's neck. Finally, I would see a single mom struggling to care for her child and felt like I dodged a bullet. It was sickening, yet it helped me cope with my choices.

Carefully, I buried my sentiments with lies… "No, I don't want children. I'm not the mom type. Why would God give me another child when I had carelessly returned my gifts to the Sender?" I dug a hole in my mind and buried both babies. But the grave could not hold them. I needed to forgive myself, but above all I wanted God to forgive me. I never asked for forgiveness because I figured it was too late. A few years later before a group of teenagers, I shared this story. As I unraveled my naked truth before them I had a vision of standing before a white porcelain sink. My hands were covered with blood from both of my babies. Water steadily flowed from the faucet. I placed my hands under the stream. The water was perfect in purity as it washed away every stain from my hands. The sink was covered in my sin; bloody red. In the blink of an eye the sink returned to a pristine white. There was no trace left of my sin. In an instant, God drained it all into a sea of forgiveness.

In school, I nicknamed myself Missy and asked all my friends to call me Missy. If I as present day MacDana could have a face-to-face conversation with Missy it would go something like this…

I understand you are seventeen and pregnant. Your parents professed this moment into your life with words spoken in anger when they said, "You will never amount to anything. It's only a matter of time before you are pregnant and useless." The words escaped their lips and followed you, keeping to the shadows, awaiting their moment of fame. The part about you being pregnant is true, but the rest I declare void. As long as you are alive, God can work with you. It is your fear and confusion which makes abortion an option. If Mom and Dad were sitting here pouring perfect love into you, your fears would disappear.

Parents were designed by God to reflect how HE loves us. Unfortunately, hurt people, hurt people. Humans often forget they are gods. As gods, humans are capable of much charity if they would only allow themselves to reach their limitless potential. God wants to tell you something Missy. Listen! He has and always will love you. Talk to Him. He is only a breath away.

CHAPTER 14

CONSUMED

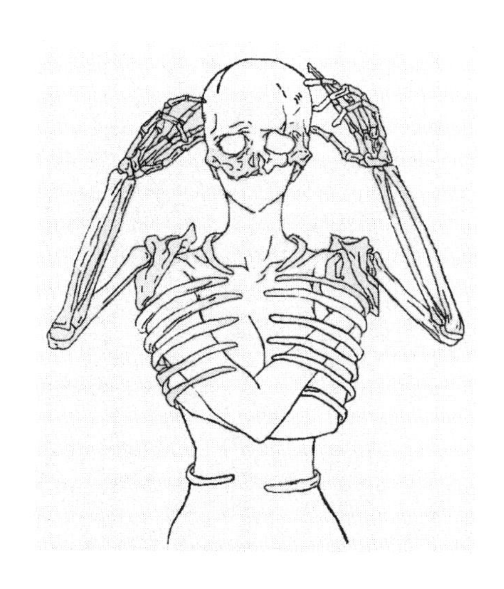

Naked I entered; in like manner I will leave.

Mirror mirror, take one last look at the joke I turned out to be.

Perhaps if I looked different, life would have been different.

Silkier hair and lighter skin.

Rounder face with flawless skin.

Thinner lips, with whiter skin.

Pointier nose rising from my skin.

A fist covered in tougher skin to smash my image in the mirror within.

See this empty womb, where my babies once grew.

Something ruptured in a place where butterflies once flew.

Heavy heart. Labored beats in the absence of hope.

Trapped. Windows sealed. Doors barred. I can't cope.

It's hard to breathe as the ceiling caves in.

I see my skeleton consuming my skin.

The walls in my mind are covered in sin.

Secrets, shame and countless regrets.

Hovering above I cannot forget, if only oh God, you would let me forget!

OR

Would you take this cup, before I take this cup, to swallow these pills and empty this cup?

Before you save or condemn my soul

Grant me the dream I longed for in this world,

My father embracing my corpse in his arms.

His tears stain my face, now he hears my song.

The wailings in my mother's lamentations

Set me free from the cage I grew up in.

Is there a place in heaven for naked girls who did not get a choice in the matter, confused by the matter

hurt by the matter

tainted by the matter,

suicidal thoughts emanating from matter?

Jesus, can you hear? Jesus, are you near? Jesus, do you care? Jesus, are you there?

JESUS! JESUS! JESUS!

"And He said unto her, ***thy sins are forgiven****."*

CHAPTER 15

NOW WHEN YOU PUT IT LIKE THAT

My mother used an interesting scale to determine a man's worth. His value increased according to the amount of money he spent on a woman. When I became a woman, I adopted her methods. Kanye West refused to call it gold digging. However, I believe it is time to call a spade a spade.

"Siri, define prostitute," I asked.

"As a noun, it means, a person, typically a woman, who engages in sexual activity for payment. Do you want to hear the remaining one?" I ignored Siri's question and read the remaining definition from my phone's screen. "A person who misuses their talents or sacrifices their self-respect for the sake of personal or financial gain."

Well, that settles it, I was a prostitute!

WHO ARE YOU CALLING A PROSTITUTE?

In July of 2003 at seventeen-years old I enlisted into the United States Air Force. In exchange for my freedom – forgive me, I meant signature - they promised me a trade and paid tuition. Months before flying to basic training a woman hired me to sell roses at nightclubs in Fort Lauderdale. I hustled in and out of dive bars and dance clubs on Las Olas Boulevard. I considered this the best job on the planet. My flowers and vendor's badge allowed me to skip every line and walk in without proof of being twenty-one or older. Even the bartenders assumed my badge cleared me for alcohol. These places were packed with single, liquored-up men who purchased my roses to impress a woman. A few roses were purchased and regifted to me. I resold them and pocketed the money. My employer had no idea the tables turned. She became my supplier, and I was paying her: #LikeABauss!

Thursday nights were slower on the strip. Fat Tuesday's had a great D.J. and a decent crowd, so I spent most of my time there. I cradled an assortment of real and artificial roses as I sang and danced to "...if you got a gun up in your waist please don't shoot up the place. WHY?" Two men stood near the bar enjoying my solo performance and caught my attention. I smiled, "clocked back in" and sauntered over. They were a contrasting duo. One stood tall, coffee with extra cream, dressed in scrub pants, t-shirt, and a baseball cap. The other, noticeably shorter, coffee with no cream, and dressed to impress. Both had a great physique, but the shorter guy looked like he did steroids. He also did most of the talking, more like showboating. His friend's scrub pants made me wonder if he just left work. *Here's an opportunity.*

His low-key persona and attentive eyes pulled me away from his loud friend. I shifted my attention and opened with my million-dollar pitch, "Hi! Would you like to buy a rose for your lady?" I tilted my head to the right, cocked my hip, pushed my chest forward and smiled. He undressed me with his eyes and I welcomed the violation.

He smiled and said, "You look very beautiful."

I smiled back. “Thank you.” He appeared genuine, but tipsy. I felt beautiful that evening. My fake pony-tail swung just right. I had fresh acrylic nails glued on earlier. And my best friend’s beige mini-skirt accentuated my butt.

“How old are you?” I lied and said twenty-two. Fooling this guy was easy. It took years to realize the other fool in the room was me. “How much for the entire bouquet?” he asked.

“About a hundred dollars.”

“What happens if you sell the entire bouquet? Will you be done working?”

“Pretty much.” He opened his wallet and handed me a crisp one-hundred-dollar bill. His friend stared at him with wide eyes.

“Thank you! Who would you like me to deliver them to?”

“The flowers are for you.”

“What… are you serious?!” My smile stretched wider and I could not hide my teeth. “Are you serious?” I asked again.

“Yes! You can spend the night dancing with me or you can double your money and continue working.” Like a true hustler, I did both.

***

He epitomized the phrase, “black don’t crack.” He tried to keep his age a secret, but the day I discovered he was twenty-five years my senior, I almost fell out of my chair. An active gym membership and playing basketball kept him in peak condition. He stood over six-feet tall and turned many heads in his worst outfit. Somewhere between his grand gesture at Fat Tuesday’s and his mysterious appeal, I got hooked.

At seventeen, I thought dating involved sneaking around to have sex. With my self-respect pushed aside, I became impressionable, vulnerable and desperate. The perfect mold for an older, affluent man looking for a good time.

I'll never forget our first date, which technically happened to be my very first date. He picked me up at 9 pm.

Let's pause this story for a second and allow me to pour some knowledge onto this page. Ladies, the only reason a man who's interested in you should arrive at your door around 9 pm is if you're going to the all-night prayer service at your local church; just kidding. But seriously, any spontaneous rendezvous after 9 or 10 pm qualifies you as a piece of tail. Don't expect a decent meal or a deep conversation. Most restaurants are scrubbing pots and washing dishes by then. Don't fall for "Girl, I just want to chill." Unless your definition for "chilling" involves sex; move on. In my culture, they call people like this an Egaré. Boo, don't be a fool.

He drove us to a fine dining establishment. Denny's. After our gourmet meal, we spent the evening at a local hotel where he introduced me to a Swiss liqueur named Goldschläger. The thin gold flakes floating in the drink fascinated me. After a few sips I became his private dancer. He sat across from me amused, calculated and curious. Curious about the young woman with low inhibition who was dancing in a hotel room before a man she barely knew. I spent the night with him, and he drove me home in the morning. Before I could exit his car he handed me several hundred dollars and told me to buy something nice. Instead of embarrassing myself and skipping to my front door like I just won the lotto, I walked away with poise, feeling like the luckiest girl in the world.

Everything he did wowed me, and he loved it. For our second date, he drove me to another hotel in the uppity town of Boca Raton. As we settled in our room he surprised me with a white gift box. I opened it to find a golden anklet. He knelt and latched it around one of my ankles and I gave him my greatest performance as a show of gratitude.

Meanwhile, within, I heard Mom's voice, "Only whores wear anklets." Later that evening I dressed for dinner, admiring my new accessory. He introduced me to prime rib, and all my taste buds exploded with pleasure.

Somewhere between frequent hookups he, too, got hooked. Weekend getaways soon turned into our thing. We soaked in hot tubs and behaved like rabbits. He kept my purse fat with cash and my lust satisfied with sex and gifts like Movado and diamond watches. He paid my car note, my rent, all-inclusive vacations, Broadway shows in New York, a mini shopping spree in Times Square, five-star restaurants, flowers sent to my jobs and little surprises under my pillow; none of it worth the T-shirt.

Besides money and sex, he cheered for me. He encouraged me to dream bigger, stay in school, and he taught me things my father failed to teach me. "You don't have to dress skimpy to feel beautiful. You are beautiful."

After my eighteenth birthday, I confessed my real age. Now that we were legally allowed to bed each other, I figured he would stay. It angered and disturbed him when he realized at forty-two years old he had slept with a teenager. But before he could even think of leaving, I manipulated his emotions like a true Jezebel. I held onto him with sex and watered-eyes to feed a constant need for attention. Skirt around wounds of abandonment, and avoid my bulging closet of demons. He stayed, and I paid a high price.

Three years in I asked, "Why haven't you introduced us to your family? Are you embarrassed by our relationship?" He'd kept me a secret from his world. *Here is the point in my story where you can call me an idiot. Go ahead. I understand.* There were many #relationshipgoals we never actualized. The closest I ever got to meeting his family was when he took me to meet his mother's tombstone at the cemetery. I respectfully introduced myself and left flowers as a parting gift. Oh wait, it gets better. In the few years we spent together, he never invited me to his house. He changed the subject whenever I inquired.

"Are you married? Is that why I can't go to your house?" I asked.

"Here we go again. You're ridiculous."

"You didn't answer the question. Are you married?"

"No, MacDana, I am NOT married. I'm tired of arguing with you about the same thing. I'm going home."

"You can end this argument right now and forever. Just take me with you."

"That is not happening. Good night."

Every holiday he disappeared, even when my birthday fell on Thanksgiving. Our time spent together continued as weekend visits. Saturday mornings I showered, dressed and waited to hear his keys outside my door. I cooked his favorite meals and paraded in lingerie in hopes he'd one day find me worthy enough to wait for at the altar. Another year went by and we continued to play house every weekend. It took four-plus years before I'd had enough.

***

Punch me. Hit me harder. Again. Hit me again.

Till I never look back and I never let you in.

Cut me. Dig in deeper. Again. Slice this piece.

Till I hate the scent of you standing close to me.

During one of his visits, he left behind an Eastbay catalog magazine for me to decide which pair of shoes I wanted. I rolled my eyes when I picked up the magazine and noticed he'd clipped his address off the back, but as I thumbed through the pages, I found a mail-in envelope with his address. "Ah-ha." I memorized it and hid the forbidden document in my top secret, Female Bureau of Investigations (FBI), underwear drawer. Several weeks passed before we resumed our argument about his secret home and secret life. This time I refused to back down, so he left without saying a word. In three days, I called him like fifty-five times, and he ignored them all. On day four of the silent treatment, Operation: *Done with This Fool* was initiated.

I shoved his address in my back pocket and flung all his items in my trunk. An hour later I pulled into his driveway and wondered who in the hell lived there.

I approached his front door and he startled me by opening it before I could ring the doorbell. "It took you long enough," he said with excitement. "Come inside." He grabbed my hand, snapping me out of pure confusion. He nervously held onto me as he explained his absence. We stepped over unfinished floor tiles and used buckets of paint as he ushered me through his home. "My beautiful MacDana, I love you, and I have nothing to hide. There is something I've been waiting to show you." He pushed open two white French doors which revealed a massive patio adorned with white Christmas lights and aromatic candles. My favorite flowers rested on a chair as a centerpiece. He led me to the arrangement as my disbelief and joy turned into tears. He embraced me and then whispered in my ear, "It's not complete yet, but you were obviously running out of patience. I left you the magazine and removed the outside address on purpose. I knew you would find the envelope. I hope you picked your sneakers; we have some work to do here. This house is my gift to you. Welcome home baby."

Nice story, right? But absurd for a non-fiction memoir. Here is what really occurred. Operation *Done with This Fool* almost got me arrested. As soon as I arrived at his address he called the police and waited for their arrival before opening the door. An officer approached, "Ma'am we are going to have to ask you to leave the property." I didn't have any bail money, so I hopped into my car. On the way home, I contemplated hurting myself for two reasons. First, to distract me from the pain in my chest. Second, to make him feel the pain in my chest. A good friend once said, "People will only treat you the way you allow them to treat you." In this situation, I found truth in her words. However, I hated MacDana too much to walk away.

"I told you my house was off limits," he said, strolling into my house several days later. We argued right into my bedroom. The following day I prayed God would remove him from my life because saying goodbye to him required divine strength. He sat in the center of my world. Both of my parents were absent, none of my siblings tried to connect, and my friends had their own lives. I spent most of my free time with him. If not with him, then on the phone with him. In between, I talked about him to anyone willing to listen. Letting go would leave behind a gaping hole I'd be forced to fill. Even though we spent most of our time arguing and I felt like his weekend fling; being alone seemed worse. He validated my existence. The crumbs of attention he fed me left me hungry, but fed me nonetheless. Being alone meant another failed relationship, and I was the common denominator.

"If money lost its value, how would you love me?" He scrunched his face in confusion, as if I'd asked him to explain the Pythagorean Theorem.

"Girl…you know I love you," he said, trying to pacify me. It didn't work.

THIS IS OVER

Finally, it happened. His storm of lies, secrets, and carelessness weathered my levee, and it broke. I held the part of me which loved him under water until it drowned to death.

"I do not want to be with you anymore." He pulled out a loaded gun and placed it on the kitchen counter. I stared at the weapon as he spun it until the barrel faced his stomach.

"Take it and shoot me."

Everything about that scene scared me, but I learned something about myself. When things get hairy, I become reckless, fearless, and faith-filled. I prayed silently for help and what followed, well, I wouldn't go so far to say God orchestrated the entire thing, but I do give God thanks for not allowing it to go over the edge.

"Get out of my house, NOW!" He grabbed his gun, tucked it away and lost his mind. Everything happened fast, but I saw it in slow motion. A chair went flying across the room, the Christmas tree followed it. I stood still and silent as ornaments and paper fell to the ground. He raised the desk chair overhead and smashed the glass table to pieces. When he broke my laptop, a woman I never met before emerged from my being, determined to kill him. I reached for the butcher's block. He ducked and dodged every knife I threw. One of them lodged into the wall behind him. He stared at it.

"You could have killed me." I threw another. He ran for the door. I grabbed a glass-vase full of flowers, opened the patio door and stood on my second-floor balcony. Just when he pulled off, I aimed at his head and threw it. SMASH! His window cracked. He stopped in the parking lot. Popped his trunk. Retrieved a lug wrench and destroyed my car's windows.

If only things had ended there…

Stalking followed. He knew my every move and showed up without permission. If he didn't show up, he called, "What were you doing at Walmart and who are your new friends?" All of it seemed strange because throughout our relationship he made it clear I meant very little to him. After changing my phone number, he started calling my new job. He did weird and creepy stuff such as splashing his cologne around my front door. One time he left giant sunflowers on my doorstep. One night I had a friend over and he started throwing pebbles at my windows. At first all of it seemed minor, but as time progressed my internal alarm said, "You are not safe."

One morning my car broke down. I took it to the mechanic.

After he assessed the damages he pulled me aside and asked, "Who did you piss off? Somebody wants you dead. With what we found in your tank your car could have easily stalled on the highway at any time. It's pure evil. I wouldn't do that to my worst enemy." The following evening a good friend helped me escape to Jacksonville, and I fell off his grid for good.

In the end I discovered my worth: priceless. Money is a piece of paper, I use to purchase things I will one day leave behind. My soul does not desire money or things. Its' only acceptable currency is love.

What I wished someone would have said to me from day one ...If an expensive car payment is forcing you to stay in a dead-end relationship; drive that piece of metal back to the dealer and walk home. If designer-wear has you hooked to a person who does not respect you; tell the devil to keep his Prada. If expensive jewels have you chained to pain; run to your local pawn shop and get paid. Take the extra money and find someone who is fighting this same battle and share your story with them over lunch. Your treat! Trust God's word: the righteous don't beg for bread, and they are ***NEVER,*** *and I mean never, forsaken.*

During that fiasco, I lost many things I thought were important. My job fired me for being a hot mess. I lost my apartment. I pawned the jewels he gave me and took back my self-respect. However, the best part of my story is Jesus. Yes, this book delineates a few hard times I endured and the drama I created. But, what you just read is another story about Jesus. When I reflect on my journey which involved physical abuse, sexual abuse, verbal abuse, and self-harm, I see grace as the paved road I walked on.

I love this definition of grace: the unearned, unmerited favor of God delivered to us by his son Christ the Lord. It is plain to see, I should not be here at this moment. Not only am I here, but I also have my right mind and best of all, I HAVE MY JOY! In between the lines of my story I see Jesus yanking me out of this, covering me from that, and telling the accuser, I love her and she belongs to me.

That is grace.

Even though I pushed Jesus aside for any and everything, He shrugged it off and waited patiently. At the moment I decided to look his way He said "Here Mac, let's switch. Give me your bag and you take mine." I handed Him my bag heavy with shame, despair and sadness and he handed me His bag. I braced myself to pick up His bag....and discovered ...it was empty.

CHAPTER 16

A LETTER TO MOM

Dear Mom,

I sit here and reflect on your childhood. What it means to grow up in a third world country with two absent parents. How a Madam adopted you and used you as her servant. How she left welts on your skin because you sang, "*Pa peny m' ti tres, pa peny m' gros tres, peny m' choux.*" (Don't comb my hair in small or big braids. Pin it up). Mom, I remember not too long ago listening with my ears pressed against the phone as you shared your story. At twelve-years-old you rummaged through your father's trash searching for food as he sat and feasted with his preferred family. You found potato skins and praised God.

Your journey continued as you boarded a crowded boat on the coast of Haiti and traveled through tumultuous conditions with hopes of landing in Miami. How you made it is beyond my understanding. I listened in awe as you shared your voyage without grief, fear, or regret. Instead, fortitude bannered over you. In a foreign land you worked in cotton fields and later studied to become a nursing assistant. With minimal wages, you provided for all your children. Today I stand reaping the benefits of your blood, sweat, and tears. You risked your life to give us and generations to come a head start.

Thank you. I will never be able to repay you, but thank you.

We grew apart over the years. I still force myself to answer when you call. With tongue in cheek we speak to each other. I am connected to you, still. As if the doctor never severed the cord. You told me not to be like you, to seek a better life for myself, and I tried. But I struggled. How? Shall I tear my face off because it looks like you? How do I lobotomize actions and inactions, yet focus on your commandments? My love for you is mixed with anger.

I wanted more for you, to make the more you wanted for me less abstract. Less out of reach. Less fantasy. More tangible. I wanted you to set the standard you drilled me with. I wanted you to make your sermon more practical. You didn't, and I questioned if you truly believed I could be better than you. If I could be the MacDana you dreamed of. The scholar and the doctor. The virgin and the saint.

Instead, I became the prisoner of your shortcomings.

So, we grew together like potted plants in a house. You grew until you touched the ceiling. Your leaves bent in submission to the walls. Your roots jutted from the soil and wrapped around you. You towered over me. I marveled at your beauty until I crashed through the ceiling and found the Son. I dug my roots through the cement and found the well. I stretched my branches until the windows broke and my leaves danced with the winds. I destroyed our house…your house. I disappointed you in search of me.

Mom, here is the thing, "As a man thinketh, so is he." To not be like you, as you asked, I also cannot be your thoughts, your hopes, dreams, and regrets. I never want to be your trophy child again. For when the ground shook, I fell. I broke. You cursed me and threw me away. I can only be who I am and I am His.

Before you and Dad conceived me, I was known as His masterpiece. Perfect in every way. There are things you will never know about me. Such as how many hairs are on my head, the tracing of the lines in my skin, the measurement of the tears I cried, how many days I have left to live, and the lives which my life story will touch. You carried me and raised me, but I do not belong to you. We belong to each other. You and I are His daughters.

I want you to know I love you.

MacDana Seleçon

God's Prodigal Daughter

CHAPTER 17
A LETTER TO DAD

Dear Dad,

When I became a woman, I compared myself to women who grew up with a father. I felt cheated. The space in my life I reserved for you stood like an abandoned home falling apart in a beautiful suburb. Throughout my childhood, I soothed my psyche by thinking, *Let's not make a big deal about his absence. I have everything I need to survive. Mom, food and shelter.* Mom tried to find a suitable replacement for you, but no one could fit your suit. I did not want another Dad. I wanted and needed you.

Loyal, but angry. I hated whomever Mom hated, including you. When you returned after no communication for ten years I reacted to the monster Mom painted of you because I had no memory of you. I hoped God did what only He could do: change your heart. But He didn't. When you showed up I was fifteen, and I needed your acknowledgments and affirmations. I figured you owed me that much. But clearly you and I were on different pages. You broke me. The little self-esteem I had vanished and promiscuity entered. And I suffered. Boys, and then men, made me feel pretty when I stood naked. Once my clothes were back on, my insecurities returned. I've often daydreamed of you telling me.... "My daughter, you are beautiful and valued far beyond treasures of gold."

I've considered for many years the daughter-daddy relationship. At weddings, my favorite dance is of the two. In a birthing suite, I cry when the father of a beautiful baby girl cries. During church service, I stare as a father kisses his daughter on her cheeks. I sit alone on park benches and get lost in between the space which separates her small hands from his big hands as they walk together.

Dad, I remember the photo you have of me. I'm dressed in a blue-top and black-capris. The picture was taken right before our junior class went to Bush Gardens. I was beautiful in that picture. I know this to be true because you kept it in your wallet. I also remember the day you picked me up from school. As I walked to your truck I realized you were holding a huge machete to scare the boys away. Embarrassing? Yes, but I understood at that moment that I'm worth fighting for. Your love knew no boundaries. I also remember when you taught me to drive your work truck. Despite it being my first time driving a manual shift and a truck, you said I could do it. I believed you. After a few instructions, you sat in the passenger seat and allowed me to drive down 441 in rush hour traffic. From then on, I knew, nothing was too big for me to conquer. Thank you for those moments. They served me well.

I love you. To hate you is to hate myself. To love you is to love the Creator. To love the Creator is to understand grace. We hardly knew each other. I wonder if you even knew what happened to me after you left. Furthermore, I don't know your childhood story; therefore, I will not dismiss it.

I am writing this letter to share my good news with you. I have given your place to another; my Father who lives in Heaven. He wrote a book declaring His unending love for me and you. His infinite affirmations rewired me. He is the catalyst in my story.

It's amazing; there is no gap when He holds my hands. He never kisses me goodbye because he is present 525,600 minutes of a year. And Dad, when I sat naked on the pavement surrounded by my blood, gasping for air He walked by and said, "Live." He covered me with his coat. He washed and dried me with his shirt. He dressed me like a royal and fed me with love. He carried me to his garden.

I am no longer the daughter you abandoned. I am the daughter He patiently waited for.

Now, I offer Him to you. Something tells me you can use a Daddy too.

Love,

Your seed,

Seleçon

CHAPTER 18

HELLO JESUS

Hello Jesus,
I need to be with you. Draw me near in this moment. Eyelids sealed I breathe you in.
Hold my hands, lace your fingers into mine.
My heart is filled with words, yet my lips are burdened to speak.
Holy Spirit, search me. Expose it all.
PLEASE...

Friend - have a seat. Allow me to rest in your love.
Deep breath in; tears pour out. Hold me tighter. Feel my tears wash your feet as virtue leaves you again and again and again.
"Oh Christ, my love. My very first love, I adore you."
Lay me down onto the arms of flying angels; hold me still as I float on air.

Descend God of old.
Engulf me in your flames, consuming fire. Purify my gold.
The blood in my veins stands still as I bend and mold to the Potter's will.
Inhale your smoke. Exhale; scorched sins
Refine my soul
Let me fall into the Jordan
Hold me under
Breathe for me Jesus. I need you to breathe for me at this moment.

Living waters permeate my pores
Hold me steady as the rivers flow over, under and through me

Stir the healing water
Call my name, and I will rise
Extend your hand. It is time for me to dance on the waters
This dance is dedicated to you, my beloved is mine, and I am His
Blow mighty, breath of God
Let the strands of my hair dance behind me
As I spin with my arms outstretched; tears of joy fall from my life
My feet glide to a new song, a new instrument, a new melody

Adorn my feet with jewels of peace
Whiten my garment with glory
Crown me Oh Bridegroom, crown me with gold from My Father's Throne

Dance with me on the water as heavenly hosts move the clouds to see, mountains bellow in song and rocks roar with praise for You, dancing with me.

The bride and the bridegroom dance at last.

Se Leçon

There were many. I learned on this journey, saying you forgive is easier than forgiving. Just like saying I love you is easier than loving. Forgiveness begins with acceptance that you too have been forgiven. Forgiven for things you knowingly did wrong and things you unknowingly did wrong. Most of us do not fully understand this gift from God. He gave His one and only Son for all our sins so we can be made righteous through him. We were forgiven before we were born. If we could only accept that. We're unfamiliar with this type of Love on the account of the people in our lives. I'm not going to sit here and lie to you; I'm still trying to understand this gift of exoneration myself.

There are two recurrent emotions found amongst child abuse survivors: shame and the inability to trust. Shame due to the unfortunate situation of being dehumanized. Loss of trust because our trust in how things are supposed to be was drastically altered. After self-exploration and coming across Luke 7:48, "And He said unto her, your sins are forgiven," I meditated on the significance of forgiving. I found that any unforgiveness blocks healing and compassion; our capacity to love.

Healing is a journey not a destination. It comes in different packages. Sometimes it is presented in a new friendship, moving to a new state, a new hobby, new passion, hiking a trail in San Mateo, CA, spending Christmas with a new family, diving off a cliff in Maui, or writing a book. Most of all is to realize, you have the power to grow and make something great out of pain and suffering. For me, it's The Luke Movement (TLM). Where our goal is to be a bridge to freedom for those suffering or who have suffered from child abuse. We foster healing, change, progression and awareness by advocating self-love and transparency. We also seek to direct those in need of resources for treatment and prevention. Visit: www.thelukemovement.com for more info and support.

Just as healing is a process, so is forgiveness. When they are ready, child abuse survivors must start forgiving themselves first. It's no easy feat. I'm still learning. I'm learning to love myself and extend forgiveness to those who have wronged me. Some wounds require our minds to be rewired. The way we see ourselves in this world is erroneous. This might take time but we must be kind to ourselves and make room for personal growth. Everyone is traveling down the road of recovery. Before I go I leave you with the words of Desmond Tutu, "a person is a person through other persons." You are not alone and I pray my story empowers you to initiate or continue your journey.

ACKNOWLEDGMENTS

To Prophetess Ralna Smith and Prophet Accius Smith, thank you. Your family welcomed me into your home after I lost so much. You allowed me time to collect myself and I wrote this entire book. From the depths of my heart, thank you. May God continue to use your ministry to guide many others into the purpose our Father has for them.

To Four Pack, aka Dawine Yoshioka, aka my sister, sent by a loving God, thank you boo. I love you. Thank you for spending the last four years editing with me. Thank you for your research. Thank you for being so honest. Thank you for being passionate when I was scared. Thank you for not giving up on me. Thank you for the pep talks. Everyone needs one person to hold their arms up when they get tired. Not only did you hold my arms up, but you also pulled me and pushed me. Sometimes you carried my passion until I had the guts to pick it up again. You are a gift. I bless the day I met you.

Thank you, Miranda Romero aka My Boo, for the kind words you spoke at a table amongst our friends. You called me one of your favorite writers. I never imagined anyone would ever say that to me. Thank you for welcoming me into your family. You are my favorite director. Thank you for an awesome book trailer. You made this book your baby and gave it a beautiful welcome onto the big screen. Thank you and I love you for making some of my wildest dreams come true.

Thank you *Cuz* (Johanne Talleyrand). Your love and support means so much to me. You have been constant throughout the years.

Thank you to everyone who asked, "When will I get to read your book?" Accountability!

Thank you to everyone who prayed for me. I love you.

Thank you Miguel Ruddock (UX designer, mentor, coach and friend). You are an amazing talent. It started as Project Freedom/ Project LK 7:48. Now we have The Luke Movement. Google is blessed to have you on board (wink, wink). I am honored to call you friend.

Thank you to Mariah Dixon for the designing the book cover and the beautiful drawing. I love you so much, and I am extremely proud to be your Aunty.

Thank you to The Luke Movement. Thank you, J Rollers Productions, for such an awesome book trailer. Thank you to Channon Prescott (extraordinary mother and human being), Kailynn Johnson (my superstar), Emmanuel Douge (how will I ever repay you), Quinese Atkins (a real one), Brandon Romero (my brother), Aliyah Jones (my sister), Tracy Lee Martin (awesome cinematographer), Lindsay Mahley (I love my manager), Jenn Goddard (phenomenal woman) and Elijah Booker (what a joy to work with you) and Dolce the dog.

To my Number one, my Everything, my Rock, my Life, my Reason, my King, my Joy, my Love, my Anchor, my Wind, my Peace, my Jesus, thank you, thank you, thank you. You are the best Daddy a girl can ask for. You rock! I love you so much. Thank you for walking with me on this journey. You are the best therapist a daughter can ask for. I feel so much lighter now because of you. Daddy, please get this book into the hands of every person who can relate. Do for them what you did for me: heal their broken heart.

Luke 7:48: Then He said to her, “Your sins are forgiven.”

Luke 5: 20: He said to him, “Man your sins are forgiven you.”

To contact MacDana Seleçon, write her at:

P.O. Box 344

Pinole, CA 94564

Or visit: www.TheLukeMovement.com